Lecture Notes
in Business Information Processing   86

Series Editors

Wil van der Aalst
Eindhoven Technical University, The Netherlands
John Mylopoulos
University of Trento, Italy
Michael Rosemann
Queensland University of Technology, Brisbane, Qld, Australia
Michael J. Shaw
University of Illinois, Urbana-Champaign, IL, USA
Clemens Szyperski
Microsoft Research, Redmond, WA, USA

Hannu Salmela
Anna Sell (Eds.)

Nordic Contributions in IS Research

Second Scandinavian Conference
on Information Systems, SCIS 2011
Turku, Finland, August 16-19, 2011
Proceedings

 Springer

Volume Editors

Hannu Salmela
University of Turku
School of Economics
Department of Management
Rehtorinpellonkatu 3
0500 Turku, Finland
E-mail: hannu.salmela@utu.fi

Anna Sell
Åbo Akademi University
Department of Information Technologies / IAMSR
Joukahainengatan 3-5 A
20520 Åbo, Finland
E-mail: anna.sell@abo.fi

ISSN 1865-1348   e-ISSN 1865-1356
ISBN 978-3-642-22765-3   ISBN 978-3-642-22766-0 (eBook)
DOI 10.1007/978-3-642-22766-0
Springer Heidelberg Dordrecht London New York

Library of Congress Control Number: 2011932689

ACM Computing Classification (1998): J.1, H.4.1, H.3.5, K.6, D.2

Typesetting: Camera-ready by author, data conversion by Scientific Publishing Services, Chennai, India

Printed on acid-free paper

Springer is part of Springer Science+Business Media (www.springer.com)

Preface
ICT of Culture – Culture of ICT

During the 21st century our society, culture and personal lives will be deeply influenced by advances in information and communication technology. Social media and social virtual worlds have already started transforming individuals from passive information consumers to active creators and distributors of information, knowledge and arts. We can already play with the idea that our technological capability will enable us to digitize everything that anyone has ever said and store it on Internet servers. How does all this affect our society and culture? How should the media industry and other companies capitalize on the new empowered consumer? How does this transformation change our concept of the welfare society?

This transformation will also affect the culture of the IS profession. IT is not created in a vacuum or designed somewhere outside our society. The new applications of ICT are increasingly a product of the surrounding society and culture. Furthermore, the cultural context where the IS development takes place is becoming increasingly diverse. Implementation of applications and practices of their use takes place in groups that involve members from different national, organizational and professional sub-cultures. The development is increasingly driven by professionals from other fields and even by consumers. How can we manage and take advantage of this cultural diversity in our development teams? What are the challenges that different cultural backgrounds create in the teams that plan, design and implement new applications?

Scandinavian researchers are well positioned to study the cultural impacts of the new technologies. Scandinavian countries are among the first ones to adopt the latest information technologies. In some areas we have been clearly leading the technological development. But the globalization of customer industries and the relatively high cost of labor have meant that the IS industry in Scandinavia has also been transformed into a globally networked and culturally diverse industry.

To promote discussion between authors of research papers and keynote speeches, SCIS 2011 invited contributions that address the cultural impact of the latest technologies, i.e., social software and intelligent data retrieval systems. We also welcomed papers that address cross-cultural issues in the IS profession itself. The resulting mix of papers in the proceedings also reflects these issues.

The keynote speech by Robert Picard opened the discussion on the cultural impacts of the latest technology with the title "Strategic Uses of Social Media for Businesses." The business use of social media is addressed in papers that investigate the role of virtual worlds in the evolution of a co-creation design culture (Molka-Danielsen) and in an empirical paper that addresses how globally distributed Danish and Indian engineers co-construct and reconfigure a shared socio-technical collaborative space (Bjørn). Papers also present empirical research material on the reasons for continuous use of social media among teenagers (Mäntymäki), and difficulties that students have experienced in exchanging socio-emotional aspects and in developing shared concepts when using multilingual communication systems (Yasuoka and Bjørn). A "lazy-user model" is proposed as an alternative to the traditional acceptance models in explaining users' adoption of the latest technologies (Collan and Tétard).

The theme of intelligent data retrieval is addressed in two papers, which investigate the consequences of increasing amounts of information to consumers and decision makers. Observations in an oil and gas company suggest that even if such systems enable decision makers to retrieve and combine information from multiple sources, providing proof that the information is correct and can be used as a basis of actions remains a challenge (Hjelle and Monteiro). In health care it is predicted that the use of intelligent health systems by consumers – rather than health care professionals – may fundamentally change the practices in the entire health service system (Lahtiranta).

The third theme, cultural changes in the IS profession, was opened with a keynote speech by Robert Galliers with the title "Paradox Regained: Information Systems in the Age of Globality." Research papers address cross-cultural issues between different organizations, between business and IS professions and between national cultures. One of the papers conceptualizes and describes the IOS planning practices of three multinational manufacturing companies (Mäkipää). Observations collected from a Swedish bank suggest that maintenance organizations should be able to link business solutions and IT solutions, thus leading to new roles for both business users and IS personnel (Nordström, Axelsson and Melin). Finally, a literature review summarizes prior research results on the role that cultural differences play in different phases of IT offshoring (Lin).

As the Scandinavian Conference on Information Systems is a young conference, organized now for the second time, the concept is still far from mature. The conference already has a high-quality conference board. The response from the senior IS researchers in Scandinavia to participate in the conference board was very positive, committed and supportive. The quality of review statements in many cases was comparable to any conference in the field of information systems.

Further work is, however, clearly needed in making the conference more attractive to potential authors. The total number of submissions was only 17, which is clearly too small for any conference. Although SCIS will have to consider very carefully its target groups, it seems likely that at least in the beginning SCIS will be dependent on submissions from Scandinavia. SCIS should become a place for Scandinavian IS scholars to receive high-quality review comments for manuscripts that they aim to submit later to a journal.

We thank all the authors – not only those whose paper was accepted – for submitting their contributions. We would also like to thank the reviewers for their excellent efforts.

The idea of culture as a theme for the SCIS 2011 came from the conference venue – Turku is the cultural capital of Europe in the year 2011. We hope that the SCIS/IRIS conference will become an enjoyable and memorable cultural event for all conference participants.

June 2011   Hannu Salmela

Organization

Program Chairs

Hannu Salmela   University of Turku, Finland
Mikko Ruohonen   University of Tampere, Finland
Christer Carlsson   Åbo Akademi, Finland

SCIS 2011 Committee

Karin Axelsson, Sweden   Jan Ljungberg, Sweden
Jacob Bardram, Denmark   Kalle Lyytinen, Finland
Birgitta Bergvall-Kåreborn, Sweden   Lars Mathiassen, Denmark
Pernille Bertelsen, Denmark   Ulf Melin, Sweden
Pernille Bjørn Rasmussen, Denmark   Anita Mirijamdotter, Sweden
Claus Bossen, Denmark   Preben Mogensen, Denmark
Tone Bratteteig, Norway   Judith Molka-Danielsen, Norway
Mikael Collan, Finland   Eric Monteiro, Norway
Jan Damsgaard, Denmark   Bjørn Erik Munkvold, Norway
Gunnar Ellingsen, Norway   Jacob Nørberg, Denmark
Kim Halskov, Denmark   Samuli Pekkola, Finland
Erling Havn, Denmark   Anne Persson, Sweden
Karin Hedström, Sweden   Tero Päivärinta, Finland
Ola Henfridsson, Sweden   Tapio Reponen, Finland
Jonny Holmström, Sweden   Matti Rossi, Finland
Helena Holmström Olsson, Sweden   Jesper Simonsen, Denmark
Pertti Järvinen, Finland   Erik Stolterman, Denmark
Anne Marie Kastrup, Denmark   Lars Svensson, Sweden
Fredrik Karlsson, Sweden   Carsten Sørensen, Denmark
Finn Kensing, Denmark   Bjørnar Tessem, Norway
Erkki Koponen, Finland   Virpi Tuunainen, Finland
Pernille Kræmmergaard, Denmark   Pirkko Walden, Finland
John Krogstie, Norway   Liisa von Hellens, Finland
Mogens Kühn Pedersen, Denmark   Pär Ågerfalk, Sweden
Katarina Lindblad-Gidlund, Sweden

Table of Contents

XII   Table of Contents

Strategic Uses of Social Media for Businesses

Robert G. Picard

University of Oxford

Social media present businesses with many opportunities for interacting with customers, potential customers, and other stakeholders. Company sponsored blogs, forums, and wikis and uses of Facebook, LinkedIn and Twitter create new ways for companies to engage in a wide variety of activities ranging from product development to direct sales and marketing.

Because they rely on web and mobile platforms already in place, their technical and distribution costs are relatively low and easily scalable because the infrastructure is provided and paid for by others. They do, however, require investments of company effort and personnel time that are costly but can be cost effective if used strategically and performance is measured and improved.

Many companies are now using social media for brand building, customer loyalty, product improvement, testing ideas, immediate sales, investor relations, and other purposes that are served with conversations with customers and other users and businesses in their value chains. Many firms operate multiple social media functions aimed at different people and groups with whom they interact such as customers, retailers, developers, etc.

It must be recognized that not all social media are equally effective for all types of companies or strategic functions so each platform and use needs to be driven by strategy, a clear understanding of what the company is trying to achieve, and with what types of persons it is trying to interact.

Concurrently, firms need to establish performance metrics to ensure performance in meeting those strategic purposes. These include benefits measured through effects on brand value, sales, and idea generation, as well as user measures such as fans, followers, number driven to other company platforms through click throughs, etc. On top of this clear cost allocation is necessary to determine with the extent to which desired returns on investments are being achieved and at what cost.

The presentation suggests ways for conceptualizing and developing strategy for uses of social media and ensuring that its uses serve clear business purposes with firms and organisations.

H. Salmela and A. Sell (Eds.): SCIS 2011, LNBIP 86, p. 1, 2011.
© Springer-Verlag Berlin Heidelberg 2011

Paradox Regained: Information Systems in the Age of Globality

Robert D. Galliers

Bentley University

"No culture can live if it attempts to be exclusive"
Mohandas Karamchand Gandhi (2nd October, 1869 – 30th January, 1948)

I take as my text for this keynote presentation, the above quote from Mahatma Gandhi. I shall attempt to apply Gandhi's sentiment to the field of Information Systems – a field that I perceive to be quintessentially global in its reach and traditions, and quintessentially trans-disciplinary in its nature – and, importantly, for its future well-being. I find it paradoxical that the field has its adherents who wish to focus our attention solely on the information technology artefact itself, often seeing the field purely in design terms; I find it equally paradoxical that the field's gate keepers often view quality research from a limited, parochial perspective.

I might also have quoted from Simone de Beauvior's "masterpiece" (sic.), *The Second Sex*:

She stands before man not as a subject but as an object paradoxically endured with subjectivity; she takes herself simultaneously as Self and as Other, a contradiction that entails baffling consequences.

Thus, paradox and irony will co-exist – interwoven, marbled – throughout my text, in the hope of evoking interest and action with a view to regaining the promise of a field that is in danger of being subsumed by managerialist, "best practice" (sic.) "solutions" (sic.) and prescriptions that limit our understanding of the mutually constituted, complex interplay and interpretation of human being and machine. The context for my treatment of the field is global; it is not limited – necessarily – to individual, or group, or organisation(s) or market, but inclusive of societal and ethical considerations.

In line with the common definition of paradox as something that is seemingly absurd or self-contradictory, I shall argue for a more nuanced, multi-faceted, and at times contradictory stance when viewing information systems – in multifarious contexts and often widely differing circumstances. I use Beck's (2000) term "globality" as opposed to "globalism" to highlight the paradox of globalisation, namely, the growing and crucial importance of a deep appreciation of local contexts, traditions and cultures.

By following this line of argumentation, I hope to contribute to a key theme of the conference, namely, that of cross-cultural issues in the study of, and development of, information systems. I do so from a more macro-level perspective: a global consideration of the developing field of Information Systems itself.

H. Salmela and A. Sell (Eds.): SCIS 2011, LNBIP 86, p. 2, 2011.

Exploring the Role of Virtual Worlds in the Evolution of a Co-creation Design Culture

Judith Molka-Danielsen

Molde University College, Department of Economy, Informatics and Social Sciences,
Britvn 2, 6402 Molde Norway
J.Molka-Danielsen@himolde.no

Abstract. A culture of co-creation in the design of services and products has emerged in global societies based on the recent pervasiveness of social media. The concept of co-creation design constitutes that individual members of communities engage in and contribute to products and services creation, along with organizational members. A relatively recent type of social media platform has been the availability of virtual worlds for co-creation design. Virtual worlds offer a three dimensional, interactive, persistent virtual environment for social interaction and collaborative design of content. This paper explores the concept of co-creation design in social media. Further it examines what more can be done with virtual worlds and how these can contribute to the evolution of the co-creation design culture. Finally we outline research questions and suggest a methodological approach to the study of co-creation design in social virtual worlds.

Keywords: co-creation design, social media, virtual worlds.

1 Introduction

Co-creation design approach is recent and increasingly applied practice to the design of services or products. Through its application in our modern global society we see the emergence of new economic models in business. It can be derived that a co-creation design culture has evolved through changes of individuals in our global society, changes in the availability and affordances of technologies, and in the uses of these technologies in particular social media technologies. In this study co-creation is defined as a design process where individual members of communities engage in and contribute to products and services creation, along with organizational members. An example of a social media platform that supports co-creation design is Facebook™ where organizational members and individual members both contribute to and benefit from content creation.

Virtual worlds (VW) are information communication technology (ICT) based environments that are a type of social media in that VW support member representation, persistent presence and allow members to interact with each other and software agents. As such, VW are viewed in this study as social media that support the concept of co-presence. The concept of co-presence has evolved and is presented in the literature review. But briefly, it is the perception of sharing a "space" simultaneously with others.

H. Salmela and A. Sell (Eds.): SCIS 2011, LNBIP 86, pp. 3–15, 2011.

People acting through the metaphor of a real world, have reported an immersive quality to VW [1]. Uses of VW have been documented to be engaging for participants in activities such as education and learning [2]. In business cultures, research has identified numerous ways in which virtual worlds have been applied by profit and non-profit organizations, these include: marketing, customization of products, virtual markets, communication in customer support, consumer research, innovation in concept creation, teaching and learning, and recruitment [3][4][5]. Given this background, how do virtual worlds contribute to the evolution of the co-creation design culture? How can features of the co-creation design model be better supported within virtual worlds? Do virtual worlds have the potential to enhance co-created value? This article will first present a literature review on co-creation design practice and its impact on society. The second part of the literature review provides definitions and gives example of the concept of virtual worlds as a social media. Next we explore the possibilities of co-creation design within virtual worlds, to address the questions above; we outline the affordances of VW and suggest its impact on business cultures in service and product design. Lastly, we outline approaches for research for co-creation design in social virtual worlds.

2   Literature Review and Theoretical Background

Van Dijk [6] defines a "network society" as one in which social and media network technologies shapes organizational structures at individual, organizational and societal levels, where the organization of groups and communities ('masses') are organized in physical co-presence. Through growing availability and pervasiveness of digital technologies the concept of co-presence has evolved, so that people can participate in activities that go beyond their physical boundaries. Wellman [7] introduces the idea of "network individualism", where he explains that individuals' interests were formerly established by geographic boundaries. But through social media these interests can extend beyond physical boundaries. That is through digital connectivity people with similar interests can connect regardless of their physical locations, and further can explore interests in multiple digital locations. This leads to more choices and opportunities for how individuals can act within society.

One of the structures of society is the business environment. In work by [8] on the co-creation of value, he lays the foundational argument that there are no static business environments. People in society change in that the behaviors and norms of younger generations are no longer the same as older generations. A study by Forrester Research points out, for example, that younger generation users of Internet are more involved in content creation activities than those of older generations [9]. The factors of new technologies, changes in people behavior and new choices, all contribute to a changing economy, as pointed out by [10]. They describe the historical progression of our economy, from agricultural (commodities), industrial (goods production), service economy, to the emergence of an experience based economy that has the goal to differentiate services into experiences. In an experience based economy value is derived from a "product or service" that is intangible and is "in the moment" experienced content. Figure 1 depicts four types of experience where customer value is realized in the consumption of the experience. There are two axes in Figure 1. The horizontal axis depicts the degree of activity of the consumer along a continuum from passive participation to active participation in the consumption of the experienced based product. The vertical axis depicts a continuum of the way information is synthesized. If absorbed, the consumer may be of a state of mind that they do not expect to contribute to the design process. They feel that the product is something outside of their own action domain. However, if immersed, the consumer may feel themselves as part of the product. As such there are less clear boundaries between the individual and the surrounding environment.

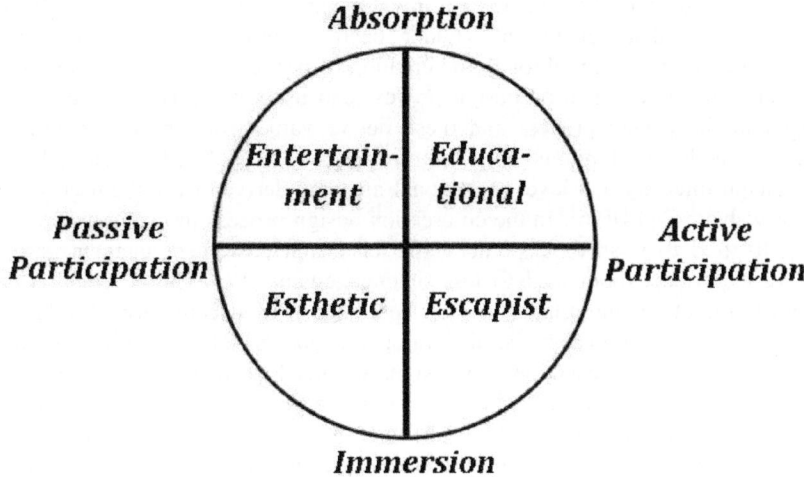

Fig. 1. Four types of experience where customer value are realized in the consumption [10]

The four experiences are:

- Educational – the consumer increases skills and knowledge through absorbing information presented in an interactive way
- Escapist – the consumer is an active participant in the experience who shapes events
- Esthetic – the consumer values being in a sensory rich environment
- Entertainment – the consumer's attention is occupied by the experience offering

The consumer may value multiple types of experience in the same product or service. Others explain, experience is "the content of direct observation or participation in an event, specifically in a co-creation process" [11, p. 161][12].

2.1 Co-creation Design

As stated earlier, the concept of co-creation design constitutes that individual members of communities engage in and contribute to products and services creation, along with organizational members. The motivation for participating in co-creation design efforts are that individual and organizational members each benefits from the co-created value that results of the contributions within the shared media. The idea of individuals contributing to innovation processes began with concepts of user innovation, where users that experience needs in the market can identify new trends and new needs [13] and "co-creation" as a systematic way for organizations to identify lead users and involve them in the creation process [14]. Organizational contribution to the co-creation is pointed out by [15]. In their study of organizations 80% have introduced user-generated content websites within the last three years and 50% indicated that they would increase investments in such websites in 2009. Organizations are spurred by recognition of benefits in the involvement of customers in co-creation design. This includes a development of better market insight, brand awareness and idea generation. Older business models have focused on the organization gaining value through the creation of products and services and sales to customers. In the co-creation design process end users or individual customers are engaged in the design process and these derive value from the experience in the process. As [8, p.3] points out, "user experience is defined as an individual's involvement intensity and level of personal meaning derived from the user-generated content websites" [14][16]. In the co-creation design process the value for customers is directly tied to positive customer experience and customer engagement. While, negative experiences can lead to loss of engagement [17]. The co-creation design process is therefore interrelated to the experienced based economy. If value is not generated on a continual basis, the value disappears. The organization in such economy must involve customers in design, and needs to encourage a constant flow of experiences and create incentives for use and participation in the community and shared experiences. One may point to the open source developer communities, where the users develop content, and the organization contributes with service support for the shared media. Several specific examples are Facebook, YouTube, and Flickr organizations and associated communities. The challenges of organizations within such communities arise in their need to create individual relationships with the contributing members. There must be incentive for individual investment. And as such the relationship between organization and individuals must address issues of autonomy, participation in the decision making process, and opportunities for member growth and skills acquisitions [8].

2.2 Virtual Worlds as Social Media

Virtual worlds are a special type of social media [5]. Internet-based applications built on the technological foundation of Web 2.0 and that allow the creation and exchange of user generated content are called "social media" according to [18, p.61]. Examples beyond the previously mentioned include Twitter, MySpace and collaborative projects such as Wikipedia. Points that VW have in common with Web 2.0 applications is that they are created, maintained and shared (often freely) by the uses of the social media often considered a community. According to [18], however, VW are a social media but have characteristics which differentiate them from other social media. These are first, VW allow users to interact with others in real time in a seemingly personal (although not identical to real life) "face-to-face" format. Most content on other media (e.g. Facebook) are typically consumed with time delay. Second, users in virtual worlds can create customized virtual self-presentations that are represented through characters called "avatars". This representation can be very flexible allowing the avatar to appear quite like the member or very different. Finally, the previously mentioned applications allow for collaboration in two dimensions, while virtual environments support three dimensional sharing of virtual elements.

Virtual worlds applications also fall under several subcategories. The virtual game (e.g. World of Warcraft) also shares the characteristics just listed, however, the applications of games usually have a game oriented goals and rule sets and limit participant behaviors to the rule set. A second category of virtual worlds as social media is the social mediated platform that does not impose restrictions on member behavior. The primary example of the social virtual world is Second Life (SL). SL is characterized as such, because it can support in-worlds societies or cultures, and does support the cultural construct of an economy. In addition the economy interacts with real life economies, in that currency generated in the virtual world can be exchanged for real life currencies. In February 2011, 1 Euro equated to 300 Linden dollars (See: http://moneyslex.com/exchange_rates.php).   Second Life is the most widely adopted of the social virtual worlds, and has been the platform of much of the following reported research.

3   Co-creation Design within Virtual Worlds: Affordances and Future Scenarios

In this section we explore the possibilities of co-creation design within VW, outline the affordances of VW and suggest its impact on business culture. As introduced in Section 2, the main affordances of VW are: real-time social interactions, flexibility of identity and design of virtual objects, and collaboration within a 3D representation. These characteristics have been reported to support immersive behavior and increased activities by members.

The affordance of real-time social interaction is defined as "feedback" by [1]. They define this as face-to-face synchronous communication. They also refer to [19] stating it is the ability of the medium to provide immediate feedback.

These [19] also define, a basis for flexibility of identity and design, is a multiplicity of cues and channels, or the ability of the medium to transmit cues (e.g. body language, or voice tone). [1] further refers to the concept of flexibility of identity as personalization or the ability to render people through clothing and avatar appearance.

The affordances to collaborate within a 3D representation is described in [1] schema as capabilities for interactivity (the ability to share and modify content collaborative, such as documents or 3D objects), capability for mobility that is the ability to move about to different virtual locations together, (by e.g. walking, flying or teleporting), and the affordance of the immediacy of artifacts (e.g. the ability to create artifacts in the forms of text, images, 3D models, 3D objects) that can be jointly shared in the 3D virtual space.

We suggest the main impact of the VW on design processes is that it should support innovative processes through support of a growing business culture both within SL and in association with organizations operating outside of SL. That is the real-time nature of the interactions in virtual worlds make members feel like they are sharing a physical space, and communicating with other members who are really "there" or present. The feeling of presence or a persistence of state can lead to increased interest in a shared activity.

Flexibility in co-creation design presents the possibility to create engaging experiences beyond those supported in 2D social media. Some have tried to gauge the quality of the co-creation design experience (an outcome of the co-creation design process), by the term "compelling" [11]. They identify that quality is evaluated by how compelling the experience is in terms of how enjoyable or engaging it was. The highest quality experiences are therefore drivers that motivate the members to keep on co-creating - facilitating a state of flow, and so remain on-going contributors to the experience [20][21].

Despite such perceived affordances of virtual worlds to support the creation of innovative experiences by its members, few cases have been documented to show co-created design. The contributions have to a large extent been by individuals or have involved organizations in contrived experiments.

For example one study describes avatars co-creation experience for contributing to the design of corporate virtual islands called "sims". The study concluded that when participants experienced a fun an intrinsically motivating design experience that they participated more intensely [11]. The participants were presented with an immersive 3D environment with stimuli of 3D objects to frame a given problem. In their "Green ideation quest" they included a scenario with objects including a coal plant, oil pump and atomic reactor to make the environment give a "dirty" impression. The participants were to act in a game where they would address word associations, knowledge questions and sentence completion tasks. While the study concluded the importance of involving avatars in the product development process, the empirical study was only based on the Green ideation quest where no commercial organization was involved.

There have been a few early adopter organizations of virtual worlds. Some noted including those identified by [21] are:

- Academia – a large number of universities
- Health/Pharmacy – AstraZeneca, Johnsen & Johnsen, Kaiser, Becton Dickson
- High Tech: IBM, Cisco, Intel, Microsoft, Sun
- Government: NOAA, NASA, DoD (US), Swedish Virtual Embassy (SE)
- Oil Industry: BP, Chevron, Statoil
- Finance: DnB (bank, Norway)
- Public Media: NRK (broadcasting, Norway)

The virtual presence of these organziations has been used largely to support knowledge sharing among an interested global community to include activities such as: meetings, conferences, collaborative 3D data visualization, collaborative design & prototyping, business activity rehearsal, and human resource management. It is not documented to what extent a co-creation design process has been used to create the experiences or virtual events hosted by these organizations. One observation we can make however, is there has been a lack of majority adoption of virtual worlds by organizations. The reason for lagging wide spread adoption of virtual worlds by organizations according to [22] is that "Pragmatist don't trust visionaries as references." There is a great difference in the belief systems of visionaries and pragmatist. While the visionaries "think big" and "go it alone", the pragmatist prefer to "manage expectations", "take a wait-and-see attitude" and "think visionaries are dangerous".

3.1   Indicative Experiences in Co-creation Design

There are few descriptive case studies involving Second Life in terms of designs for learning. Our research group has begun with a process of critical evaluation of learning designs in VW, based on experimentation and experience [23][24][25][26]. Further we identify in (Panichi, et al, 2010) that the immersive nature of Second Life suggests addressing learner participation in terms of learner engagement with the environment from an ecological perspective [27][28].   In [29] we explain the importance of this theory in light of co-creative design. We state:

> "The ecological model sees systems as open, complex and adaptive, comprising elements that are dynamic and interdependent. According to this model, all learning is situated in an environment and, as such is contextualized. In this view of learning, for example, the learner not only is part of the environment but is also one of the variables in determining subject matter and the outcome of learning and teaching. Similarly, all socio-culturally organized actions act, in turn, as a resource for further action. In an ecological perspective of learning, people and the learning community are also constituent features of the environment and levels of engagement are dependent upon meaningful participation in human events involving perception, action and joint construction of meaning. Ultimately, the resources of the specific learning environment – the physical, the cognitive, the collective knowledge base, the social, the cultural, etc. – become affordances or, in other words, are "activated" via engagement." [29, p. 186]

We are describing designs for learning in language learning where value is co-created and the experience based product of knowledge is constructed through collaboration. This involves frameworks or ways of learning that are also new in the face-to-face arena. Therefore, future studies that make assessment of the learner performance and assessment of the co-created value to learners are needed.

3.2   Enabling Activities in Co-creation Design

To enable the co-creation design of experiences through virtual worlds, we think that organizations need to activate virtual world affordances to address the core challenges. Enabling activities are suggested in the matrix in Table 1. Table 1 is based loosely on the framework of [1], in that we have consolidated the description of affordances as described in Section 3. In this table we identify activities to address the challenges of co-creation design that were introduced in Section 2.1 where we refer to [8]. (Both organizations and individual participants need to derive value from the virtual experiences or events. In order to facilitate the value creation a continuing evolution of the virtual environment platform for supporting individual-to-organizational relationships must develop. For example, how does an individual member of a virtual community contribute to the design of a context or event on an organizations sim? Is there an open-access design space (often called "sandbox" in SL), and is there an authority or virtual land manager from the organization that screens ideas and perhaps implements some. Communication practices developed by open-source communities represented in virtual worlds (such as the SLOODLE community in Second Life: http://www.sloodle.org/moodle/) should be more widely publicized to private organizations, who like individuals, may also be new to virtual worlds.

Table 1. Font sizes of headings. Table captions should always be positioned *above* the tables

Virtual World Affordances / Co-Creation Challenges	Communication support in real time: •synchronous, co-presence of avatars •multimodal (visual, text, audio) representation of space , place and objects •group interactions	Flexibility in design of identity and objects: •Anonymity by choice •Richness of mediation •Mediated feedback with VW objects •Embodiment – relation between self & avatar	Collaboration within a 3D representation •Ability to share in creation and modification of content •Ability of avatars to move around in novel ways and with other avatars •Virtual economies
Support individual-to-organizational relationship	Make use of VW voice, text chat, and aspect of the VW to support one-to-one or group communications [30][31]	Provide guides, interactive assistance (through avatars or AI software), links to web pages to identify the organization; make contact information real and available when organizations wish to be represented; allow individual members to choose level of anonymity when possible	Make use of virtual workshops to unleash creativity, apply games, word associations, brainstorming [11]
Create incentive for individual investment	Create exhibition areas to show collaborative work; create expert users group with extra sim rights (incentive to help new members); Create a rating system on shared designs.	Create objects based on historical representations or real world places to create a more immersive and inspiring environment to participants	Make known that Linden Lab grants copyright ownership of creation to consumers [32]. The policy legitimatized customer as creative and collaborative rights holder.
Provide support for membership growth and skills acquisition	Provide a VW toolkit: joint authored text (GoogleDocs on a prim), shared whiteboards and streaming video boards, in-world signs, teleporters to group locations, idea-box	Provide instructional videos to instruct participants in role-play or organization related projects how to change clothes or other appearance; Post events on public calendars outside of the VW	Provide stimulating or compelling experiences through 3D interactions of the member avatars in the virtual space, with other avatars and objects (e.g. play virtual football together)

4   Research Questions and Methodology for Addressing Co-creation Design in Virtual Worlds

Some research interprets that the co-creation design process is in action and describes the very creation of the social media platform of Second Life. To quote Philip Rosedale of Linden Lab:

To me, that's the beauty of Second Life: all we've created is a platform, an almost breathed life into it. If empty world: where we got lucky is in the fact that you (users) came along and Second Life is a world at all, it's because you've created it. [33, p.4]

However, the process of co-creation design was not merely luck but was based on principles of incentive for individual creation [32]. It is more than a phenomenon in the growth of Second Life itself, although SL has also a community of members. The concept of co-creation design is a culture that exists in many communities or societies that are active within Second Life.   The business plan of organizations active in Second Life may not only involve tangible retail products but may sometimes offer experience based products and value. Examples could be found in the tourism industry, travel agencies creating virtual experience to encourage customers to come to real world locations, or perhaps receiving feedback on the design of a real life hotel as was in the case of Starwood Hotels [34]. A few questions for future research that spring to mind are how can:

- the quality of experience based on co-created value be evaluated within a social virtual world media such as Second Life
- various types of products be developed and improved through virtual worlds
- the affordances of virtual worlds enhance marketing strategies
- organizations support personalized relationships with members in virtual worlds
- incentives be provided to entice individual investment in co-creation designs
- tools for membership support and skills acquisition effecting   growth in   co-creation cultures be developed

While not all products can be sensed with all sensory attributes in virtual worlds, these platforms can still be involved in the experience of the products. As [35] point out, a customer can order a glass of wine for her avatar, and will not be able to taste or smell the wine. But, a wine tasting group can meet in a virtual world. They can exchange their knowledge and ideas, and even give feedback from real time wine tasting in the atmosphere of a social gathering. The researchers suggest that businesses should consider the attributes of their products and map out how they can be experienced and marketed appropriately and suggest applying the theory of cognitive fit [36][37].

Another theoretical lens would be to examine these questions through media richness theory [38]. The richness of a medium is dependent on the medium's capacity for immediate feedback and personalization. Services that require communication between customers and organization will benefit from richness of medium, through experiencing the product in different ways. An avatar might wear virtual running shoes, or see a picture of them; they may further see their avatar run very quickly with the shoes. All of these "views" can make different impressions.

A general design approach for the creation of co-created experienced based products might follow a Design Science Research approach [39].

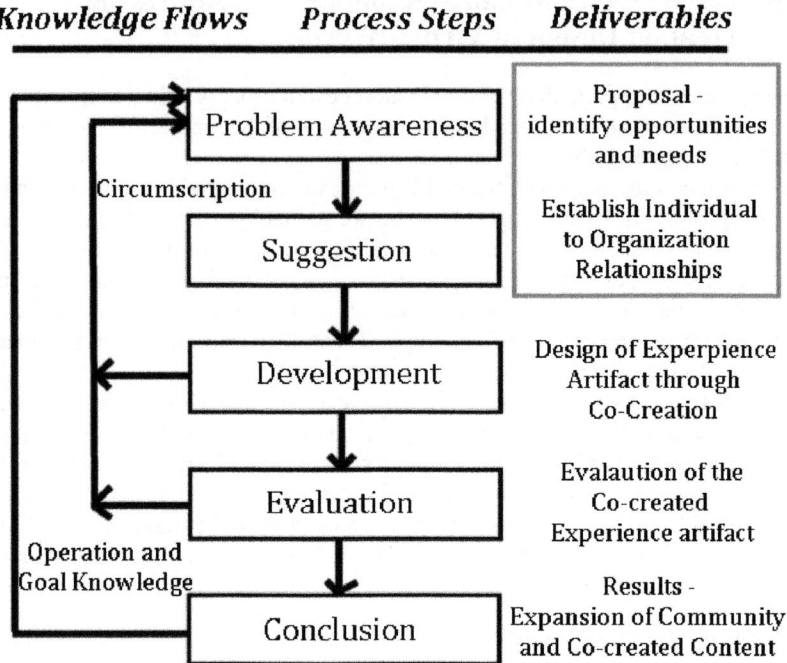

Fig. 2. Design Science Research general steps [39] as applied to Co-creation design in virtual worlds

This methodology approach is depicted in Figure 2 [39].   In a workshop for developing user innovation in Second Life, it was recommended that DSR can be used to design an artifact as DSR is a problem solving process used to develop IT artifacts [40]. The IT construct of the experience based product in this case would be the IT artifact. Through a cyclical process the experience product could be developed to gain better understanding of the design process, enactment and consumption of the experience [41][39]. The DSR process consists of five steps: problem awareness, suggestion, development, evaluation and conclusion. Figure 2 demonstrates how the DSR methodology can be applied to the design of co-created content. The design of the experience artifact will differ from the creation of more typically thought of tangible products, such as a database to support marketing. The experience artifact is continuously consumed and has different interpretations and values for different consumers. The results of the design process are therefore both changes in the co-created content but also in the community that creates it.

5   Concluding Remarks

A co-creation design culture has emerged in modern global business economies. To what extent that culture will evolve through virtual worlds is yet to be seen. While there are many examples of the practices of co-creation design in Web 2.0 social media applications, the appearance of co-creation design practices in social virtual worlds is relatively new. This paper has outlined the many affordances of virtual worlds to support a co-creation design culture. At present the impact on private organization and on business economies is very limited. It could be that co-creation design in virtual worlds will benefit future organizations by allowing customers to experience their products in multiple and rich media contexts. This article next outlined the challenges of the co-creation design process. It was suggested that more activities to address the challenges of the process are needed before the practice of it will take-off in virtual worlds. In addition the knowledge sharing approaches of successful open sources communities in virtual worlds (e.g. SLoodle) could be explored as role-models within virtual worlds and replicated by private organizations that are new to virtual worlds. Finally, it was outlined how the Design Science Research methodology can be applied to the co-creation design of experiences within virtual worlds. Some limitations of the currently popular virtual world's culture were not explored in this article. One of the limitations of to the adoption of a co-creation design process by private organizations in virtual worlds may also be influenced by the macro-culture of the most popular world of Second Life. At present many businesses do not accept Second Life as a serious place of business. The current platform may not support issues of trust building in alliances. Also the free and no-central management of behaviors in Second Life give organizations limited control over issues of privacy and security of spaces.   Finally, the centrally managed technology platform of Second Life may not be as reliable as required for some business activities. These limitations hinder its adoption and use in general, and place limitations on the evolution of the co-creation design culture on that platform. Nevertheless, we think this approach will eventually succeed in Web 3.0 technologies as it has in Web 2.0 technologies.

References

1. Davis, A., Murphy, J., Owens, D., Khazanchi, D., Zigurs, I.: Avatars, People, and Virtual Worlds: Foundations for Research in Metaverses. Journal of the Association for Information Systems 10(2), 91–117 (2009)
2. Molka-Danielsen, J., Carter, B., Richardson, D., Jæger, B.: Teaching and Learning Affectively within a Virtual Campus. Int. Journal of Networking and Virtual Organisations, Special Issue Toward Virtual Universities 6(5), 476–498 (2009)
3. Barnetta, A.: Fortune 500 companies in Second Life – Activities, their success measurement and the satisfaction level of their projects. Master thesis ETH Zürich (2009)
4. Breuer, M.: Second Life und Business in virtuellen Welten. Whitepaper (2007), http://www.pixelpark.com/de/pixelpark/_ressourcen/attachment s/publikationen/0703_White_Paper_Second_Life_e7_Pixelpark.pd f (accessed on December 3, 2009)
5. Kaplan, A.: User Participation within Virtual Worlds: Mass Customization, pp. 333–351. Springer, London (2011) ISBN 978-1-84996-489-0, http://dx.doi.org/10.1007/978-1-84996-489-0_16 (accessed)
6. Van Djik, J.: The Network Society: Social Aspects of New Media De netwerkmaastchappij, pp. 6–40. Bohn Staflen Van Loghum, Houten (1991)

7. Wellman, B.: Physical Place and Cyber Place. International Journal of Urban and Regional Research 25,2(06), 227–252 (2001)
8. Di Gangi, P.: The Co-creation of Value: Exploring Engagement Behaviors in User-generated Content Websites. In: Dissertation etd-05202010-164450, Florida State University (2010)
9. Hempel, J.: Inside Innovation in Data. In: Forrester Research Chart, Business Week, June 17 (2007),
   http://www.businessweek.com/magazine/content/07_24/b4038405.htm (accessed)
10. Pine II, B.J., Gilmore, J.H.: The Experience Economy. Harvard Business School Press, Boston (1999)
11. Kohler, T., Fueller, J., Stieger, D., Matzler, K.: Avatar-based innovation: Consequences of the virtual co-creation experience. Computers in Human Behavior 27, 160–168 (2011)
12. Takatalo, J., Nyman, G., Laaksonen, L.: Components of human experience in virtual environments. Computers in Human Behavior 24(1), 1–15 (2008)
13. von Hippel, E.: Democratizing Innovation. The MIT Press, Cambridge (2005)
14. Prahalad, C.K., Ramaswamy, V.: The future of competition: Co-creating unique value with customers. Harvard Business School Press, Boston (2004a)
15. Deloitte: Tribalization of Business Study. In: Moran, E., Asmundson, P., August, K., Openshaw, K. (eds.) Deloitte 31 (2008)
16. Prahalad, C.K.: Ramaswamy,: Co-creation experiences: The next practice in value creation. Journal of Interactive Marketing 18(3), 5–14 (2004b)
17. Wesch, M.: An Anthropological Introduction to YouTube. In: Wesch, M. (ed.), vol. 55(34). Library of Congress, USA (2008)
18. Kaplan, A.M., Haenlein, M.: Users of the world, unite! The challenges and opportunities of social media. Business Horizons 53, 59–68 (2010)
19. Daft, R., Lengel, R.: Organizational information requirements, media richness, and structural design. Management Science 32(5), 554–571 (1986)
20. Csikszentmihalyi, M.: Flow: Psychology of optimal experience. Harper & Row, New York (1990)
21. Csikszentmihalyi, M.: Creativity: Flow and the psychology of discovery and invention, 1st edn., p. 456. Harper Perennial, NewYork (2002)
22. Moore, G.: Crossing the Chasm, Strategic Business Insights. In: Whitepaper (2010),
   http://www.strategicbusinessinsights.com
23. Deutschmann, M., Panichi, L., Molka-Danielsen, J.: Designing Oral Participation in Second Life: A Comparative Study of Two Language Proficiency Courses. ReCALL 21(2), 70–90 (2009)
24. Molka-Danielsen, J., Panichi, L.: Building a Language Learning Community in a Virtual World. In: NOKOBIT (ed.) Program Committee, pp. 81–94. Tapir Akademisk Press, Trondheim (2010) ISSN 1892-0748
25. Molka-Danielsen, J., Balandin, S.: Design of a Learning Activity in Second Life: Active Teaching of Social Educators. In: Cheney, A., Sanders, R. (eds.) Teaching and Learning in 3D Immersive Worlds: Pedagogical Models and Constructivist Approaches, pp. 112–128. IGI Global (2011)
26. Deutschmann, M., Molka-Danielsen, J., Panichi, L.: Analyzing the Design of Telecollaboration in Second Life using Activity Theory. In: Cheney, A., Sanders, R. (eds.) Teaching and Learning in 3D Immersive Worlds: Pedagogical Models and Constructivist Approaches, pp. 151–167. IGI Global (2011)

27. van Lier, L.: The Ecology and Semiotics of Language Learning: a Socialcultural Perspective. Kluwer Academic Publishers, London (2004)
28. Kramsch, C.: Ecological Perspectives on Foreign Language Education. Language Teaching 41, 389–408 (2008)
29. Panichi, L., Deutschmann, M., Molka-Danielsen, J.: Virtual Worlds for Language Learning and Intercultural Exchange: Is it for Real? In: Guth, S., Helm, F. (eds.) Telecollaboration 2.0: Languages, Literacies and Intercultural Learning in the 21st Century, pp. 165–195. Peter Lang, Bern (2010) ISBN 978-3-0343-0440-5
30. Dennis, A.R., Wixom, B.H., Vandenberg, R.J.: Understanding fit and appropriation effects in group support systems via meta-analysis. MIS Quarterly 25(2) (2001)
31. Zigurs, I., Evaristo, R., Katzy, B.: Collaborative technologies for virtual project management. In: Academy of Management Executive, Washington, D.C. (2001)
32. Langenderfer, J., Kopp, S.W.: The digital technology revolution and its effect on the market for copyrighted works: Is history repeating itself? Journal of Macromarketing 24(1), 17–30 (2004)
33. Rymaszewski, M., Au, W.J., Wallace, M., Winters, C., Ondrejka, C., Batstone-Cunningham, B.: Second life: The official guide. John Wiley and Sons, Hoboken (2006)
34. Jana, R.: Starwood Hotels Explore Second Life First. In: Bloomberg Businessweek, Innovation, August 23 (2006),
    http://www.businessweek.com/innovate/content/aug2006/id20060
    823_925270.htm
35. Lui, T.-W., Piccoli, G., Ives, B.: Marketing Strategies in Virtual Worlds. The Data Base for Advances in Information Systems 38(4), 77–80 (2007)
36. Vessey, I.: Cognitive Fit: A Theory-Based Analysis of the Graphs Versus Tables Literature. Decision Sciences 22(2), 219–240 (1991)
37. Suh, K.S., Lee, Y.E.: The Effects of Virtual Reality of Consumer Learning: An Empirical Investigation. MIS Quarterly 29(4), 674–697 (2005)
38. Daft, R.L., Lengel, R.H., Trevino, L.K.: Message Equivocality, Media Selection, and Manager Performance: Implications for Information Systems. MIS Quarterly 11(3), 355–366 (1987)
39. Vaishnavi, V., Keuchler, W.: Design Research in Information Systems. Association for Information Systems, January 20 (2004),
    http://home.aisnet.org/displaycommon.cfm?an=1&subarticlenbr=
    279 (last updated August 16, 2009)
40. Spence, J. (ed.): The Researcher's Toolbox. Journal of Virtual Worlds Research 3(1) (2010)
41. Hevner, A.R., March, S.T., Park, J., Ram, S.: Design science in information systems research. Management Information Systems Quarterly 28(1), 75–106 (2004)

Co-constructing Globally Collaborative Spaces: A Conceptual Study of War Room Meetings as Spaces with Placed-Based Activities

Pernille Bjørn

IT-University of Copenhagen, Rued Langgaards Vej 7, 2300 Copenhagen S, Denmark
pbra@itu.dk

Abstract. This paper presents insights from an ethnographic study investigating how globally distributed Danish and Indian engineers co-construct and reconfigure a shared socio-technical collaborative space for global interaction. The globally collaborative space was not persistent a priori but co-constructed and reconfigured through place-based activities forming the connections between people, artifacts, and activities. Global places are temporal in nature, thus only traces of the places can persist outside the place-based activities. We show how the engineers chose to transfer their globally distributed plan into a locally tangible and persistent artifact that was useful for handling the articulation work of engineering. This move produced new challenges related to the geographical distribution of the engineers because the locally tangible plan was not globally available.

Keywords: War room, group-to-group, engineers, space, place, globally collaborative spaces, global engineering.

1 Introduction

Collaboration across time and space is increasing entering the center of attention for Information Systems (IS) research. Over the last decade, important concepts such as common ground [1], shared context [2], and trust [3] have all been linked to collaborative practices between geographically dispersed participants. Although all of these concepts are essential to understanding the basic nature of globally collaborative practices, few studies reflect on how we can conceptualize a global space for collaboration and how this conceptualization is linked to the practical enactments of people collaborating.

This paper explores the creation and re-configuration of globally collaborative room-sized spaces as they appear in real-life collaborative practices between Indian and Danish engineers. The aim of this paper is to add to the existing research on the design of room-sized technologies [4] by exploring how we can conceptualize the notion of space and place in a global collaborative setting. We look at how large-scale group-to-group collaborative global spaces are re-configured to support global interaction, and how these global spaces emerge in the enactment of technologies and human interaction. The engineers in our case enacted the global space through placed-based activities employing and reconfiguring a mixture of digital and physical

H. Salmela and A. Sell (Eds.): SCIS 2011, LNBIP 86, pp. 16–28, 2011.
© Springer-Verlag Berlin Heidelberg 2011

artifacts. The artifacts was in particular related to the articulation of team processes making team methodologies and processes visible available [5] for others to monitor and thus act accordantly. Increased visibility is only a small step towards distributed collaboration; a much larger leap is how to adopt and reconfigure new methodologies for articulation of group processes [5]. Our empirical case is a unique opportunity to study empirically how the engineers engage in co-constructing and re-configuring a globally collaborative space. Insights from this study explain how the engineers configured and reconfigured both the technical and the social aspects of their collaboration while they enacted the collaborative space connecting the two geographical localities.

We have been studying how the engineers design and reconfigure their global meeting rooms and in this paper we investigate how we can conceptualize space and place in this type of setting. We focus on both the socio-technical structures and on the enactment of the available artifacts. Drawing from the debate about on spaces and places [e.g. 6], the argument in this paper is that the globally collaborative spaces are co-constructed and reconfigured through the connections between people, artifacts, and activities. Consequently, globally collaborative *spaces* are socio-technical co-constructions that become transformed through *place-based activities* during the collaborative practices between dispersed participants. However, place-based activities are temporal in nature; thus, only traces of the space can persist outside of the meeting activities.

The paper is structured as follows. First we revisit prior research on spaces and places. Then we introduce our method and the empirical case. The analysis has two sections, each providing an account for a different setup for the global collaborative space. Then we discuss the main findings, and finally offer our conclusions.

2 Spaces and Places

Investigating collaborative spaces as entities with certain affordances for collaborative practice is an essential part of Computer Supported Cooperative Work (CSCW) research, and design of collaborative technologies has often been articulated as design of common information spaces [7, 8], as collaborative virtual environments [9], as media space [10], or as wall-scale workplaces [4]. Common information spaces (CIS) or collaborative virtual environments (CVE) are two different approaches to making it possible for the distributed actors to perceive, access, and manipulate shared information either by providing shared databases or by making the participants represented within the virtual environment. Media space is somewhat different because it is more about creating a video/audio link for informal interaction [10]. One important feature of CIS and CVE is that the "virtual" aspect of these types of desktop technologies distorts the sense of the physical space – there is no clear notion of space in the virtual [11]. Media space technology creates some kind of spatiality because the "other" becomes visibly available [10], but it is not a "shared space"; it is, rather, a peek into other peoples' spaces. The wall-scale workplaces approach takes the "space" technologies to a new level by not focusing only on bringing the real to the virtual, or vice versa. Instead, this approach takes seriously both the physical and digital artifacts and interactions, and it designs a mixed-mode space where physical objects, such as post-it notes, are transformed into digital components that can be shared across geographical distance [4]. Common to all of these technology approaches is that they are open-ended by nature, meaning that they do not stipulate how the participants should apply them in their work. Therefore, users of such systems are required to engage in shared activities in order to arrive at a shared understanding and interpretation of the meaning within these technologies.

Our empirical case can be characterized as global group-to-group collaboration where multiple actors share a common field of work and are interdependent in their individual activities when they interact through various connections, primarily within and across geographical sites. A characteristic of such collaboration is that while the entire group at each site may participate in information exchange, a range of sub-groups (both across and within sites) also interacts in parallel [5]. In such collaboration, a new type of interaction problem occurs and articulation becomes a central activity. The concept of "space between" has been suggested as a way to identify the gaps in common understanding leading to miscommunication within group-to-group collaboration [5]. Space between can be used to identify when the perspectives of participants are aligned while figuring out the extent to which coordination and articulation can bridge the gaps. It is important to point out that even though the empirical case is group-to-group collaboration, our perspective and focus on space is quite different from the space between. Whereas Mark et al. [5] investigate the space between as the connections, interdependencies, and gaps leading to common meaning misconstruction that exist within group-to-group collaboration, we investigate the co-construction of globally collaborative spaces and the re-configuring of geographical localities as they transform over time within group-to-group collaboration.

There is an important distinction between space and place. While the shared *space* is the "scheme" for the collaborative engagement – the database or the virtual environment – it is not until people begin to use the shared space, when they enact the shared space, that the interpretation work is initiated. The meaning-making process of the shared objects and artifacts is initiated in *doing* the action, and this is where the space becomes the *place*.

Space and place are two-sides of the same coin, and the concepts of place and space have been intensely debated [12]. Describing the distinction between space and place is often done by quoting Harrison and Dourish's catchy phrase: "space is the opportunity; place is the (understood) reality" [6, p. 67]. The main point is that there is a distinct difference between the design of a space (simple physical or virtual location as in the CIS or the CVE) and the design of a place (conceptualized as a location designed for human functionality) [13]. A space comprises the available artifacts, which form certain opportunities for action. Place is highly related to the human activity, which goes on in the space. Places are characterized and explicated by the construction of meaning of place through three kinds of relationships: loci, people, and events [13]. Place can be understood as a semantic tangle connecting these three [13]. Loci is "the space-places that exist (or do not) prior to the commencement of the place creation" [13, p. 108], and the meaning of place is dependent upon the people involved, the activities they do, the artifacts they encounter, and the loci. The main point here is that we cannot think about place without the activities going on in that place. A space emerges as a place through the activities people are involved in while enacting the space. If we change the people, this will transform the place – or, if we make the same people do different activities, this will transform the place. People's enactment of the socio-technical opportunities forms the place.

Related to the work in this article, this insight tells us that if we want to investigate how a globally collaborative place is constructed, we need to focus on how that space is used by particular participants when engaging in particular joint activities because this is the time were space becomes place. Put simply, we need to investigate how global spaces emerge through people's place-based activities. Also we must investigate how different people, different activities, and different artifacts transform the opportunity for collaboration at particular times.

But what about space then; how can we investigate globally collaborative spaces? Space is not just the opportunities, it is a socially constructed phenomenon [12]. The idea of spaces as socially constructed is interesting for the study of geographically distributed participants because space does not necessarily have to be linked to a particular physical location. In a study of the distributed work practices within in a wastewater plant, the authors argue that a continuum of places together constructs the space for collaboration [14]. Our focus is to understand the work practices of globally collaborative activities performed by engineers when designing spaces to create the opportunity for place-based global activities.

By studying how the globally collaborative space were constructed as connections between the geographical localities, we investigated both 1) how the collaborative space became socially constructed while 2) focusing on how the construction of space was further enacted when the geographically distributed participants became engaged in the activity of War Room meetings, thus enacting place-based activities.

3   Method

The method applied in this study was a empirical field study [15, 16]. The approach we took was to conduct observations and interviews from both the Danish and the Indian location. Moreover, we tried to become engaged with Danish engineers in their reflection about the design and re-configuration of the space by prompting on-going reflections of what was seen during informal lunches, etc. This approach allowed us to gain an understanding of the reflective nature of the practitioners when they were handling their collaborative planning practices while co-constructing the globally collaborative space for interaction.

We interviewed participants, War Room facilitators, engineers, and managers (in total, 19 people) in both Denmark and India. We observed the work practices involved in developing the War Room methodology and building the locations in both India and Denmark. Finally, we observed elleven War Room occasion each containing 4-5 meetings, two occasions from the Indian location and nine occasions from the Danish location.

Table 1. Data Sources

Data sources	Numbers/hours	Month/year
Interviews	10/6 DK-4 IN	February 2010-June 2010
Group interviews	3/2 DK-1IN	February 2010-June 2010
Interviewees in total	19/11DK-7IN	
Observations of activities in DK (excluding War Room meetings)	4 hours	May 2010-June 2010
General observations in IN (excluding War Room meetings)	3 days in Feb/5 days in Nov	February, November 2010
Observation of War Room sessions IN	2 occasion of 4-5 meetings	February, November 2010
Observation of War Room session DK	9	June, Aug, Sep, Oct 2010

4 Empirical Case

GlobalEngineering is a leading supplier of equipment and services to the global cement and minerals industries, and their main expertise is designing and building factories. GlobalEngineering employs more than 10,500 people world-wide and has a local presence in more than 40 countries. GlobalEngineering has three main locations in Denmark, India, and the United States. The engineers collaborate across geography, time, and culture when designing and building cement or minerals factories.

A project within GlobalEngineering is initiated when a client places an order for a cement factory to be designed, built, and erected in, for example, Africa or Asia. The clients are large global actors with several cement or minerals factories all over the world. GlobalEngineering then engineers the design while arranging for the factory to be erected in the location picked by the client within a particular time frame: normally 24 months.

4.1 War Room Meetings

In the last two to three years, GlobalEngineering and other western engineering companies have been pushed from the market for building cement factories inside and outside of China because Chinese companies were able to design, build, and erect standardized factories cheaper and faster. GlobalEngineering is still the leading actor in the technology for cement factories as well as in designing, building, and erecting specialized factories, but they had to optimize their processes if they wanted to keep their lead.

In early spring 2009, GlobalEngineering began to develop new concepts for how they could manage the planning practices between their specialized engineers and, in particular, between their geographically distributed sites. One of the main ideas was to implement so-called War Room meetings to support the collaborative planning practices between the approximately 300 engineers situated all over the world.

Fig. 1. War Room meeting

The main premise was to provide the individual engineer with an overview of the whole plan connected to the specialized individual tasks. In engineering a factory there are approximately 3500 individual tasks, all with dependencies and all requiring highly specialized engineering knowledge. Not knowing how the individual tasks influence the overall project, the engineers tend to put small tasks off for later, causing others to be delayed and creating "air pockets" within the plan. The War Room meetings were created to reduce these air pockets and to speed up the process. At the end of 2009, GlobalEngineering initiated three smaller projects (sub-processes of a whole factory) wherein the collaborative planning practices were handled as War Rooms; this change allowed them to do in only 16 weeks the same general engineering processes that would normally take 52 weeks. The War Room concept was a success, and in May 2010, GlobalEngineering decided to expand the concepts within the organization as well as started to think about how to design technologies to support the War Room meetings.

5   War Room Meetings: Spaces and Placed-Based Activities

GlobalEngineering have conducted War Room meetings in two distinct different types of physical setups. In the first socio-technical setup, they use their ordinary high-definition videoconferencing localities on both the Danish and the Indian site, and in the second setup, they reconfigured the Danish geographical locality to suit the War Room meeting in better ways, while leaving the setup in India the same. We will now investigate the two types of setup and reflect upon how the global spaces are constructed and enacted. We show how the construction of the spaces and places form the affordances for the socio-technical construction of the global collaboration and, in particular, how the spaces were co-constructed by place-based activities.

5.1   High-Definition Video Conferencing

The first socio-technical setup comprised two ordinary video conferencing rooms, one in Denmark and one in India. Here it is important to notice that GlobalEngineering have several ordinary videoconferencing facilities at their sites both in Denmark and in India. All employees can book these rooms, but for the War Room meetings the participants require the large physical posters, which cannot move easily. Thus, all War Room meetings were conducted in the same facilities at both sites. The rooms at both sites formed a normal size meeting room for approximately 12 people, with a large table surrounded by chairs in the middle of the room. On the walls of the geographical localities hung large brown papers (the War Room posters) for the different parts of the factory design.

5.1.1 Enacting Artifacts in Global Activities

During the War Room meetings in this type of socio-technical setup, the participants stand along the walls in the room, because the large meeting table surrounded by chairs occupies the middle of the room. On the back wall the image of the other geographical location is projected.

From the Indian geographical site, participants can see that the Danish facilitator is consulting the poster hanging on the wall located in Denmark. From the perspective of the Indian screen (see Fig. 2), the poster is placed on the wall to the right of the camera, and it is impossible to actually see what is on the poster. While the facilitator is working with the poster – moving yellow stickers around, crossing out tasks done while comparing it with the print-out plan located on the brown paper – he is speaking aloud, making it possible for the engineers in India to follow his individual work. From the Danish site the focus is on the local poster, however when looking at the screen projecting the remote location the Indian participants emerge into the collaborative space. The main role of the remote participants (not at the site where the poster is located) is in some situations to become aware of the overall status of the project, and therefore their role is to observe, while responsive when asked direct questions. The facilitator speaks out aloud while going through the yellow stickers, plans, and dependencies. In this way, the facilitator makes the information audibly available for the Indian engineers to overhear, even though it is not visually available. The role of Indian engineers is then to relate this audio information to their individual activities and speak up in the case of a changed state of the common work.

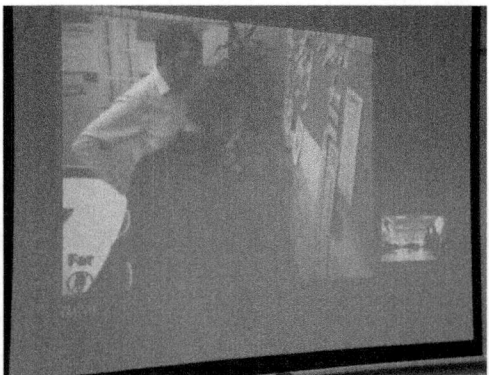

Fig. 2. The artifact is not visible from a distance

The artifacts such as the brown paper and yellow stickers become part of the placed-based globally collaborative activities when these artifacts are included in the activities conducted during the War Room. While these artifacts are part of the local collaborative space in Denmark, they only become part of the globally collaborative space when enacted by the participants through place-based activities mediated by audio.

5.1.2 Including People in the Global Activities

During meetings in the high-definition video conferencing rooms including people into the global space is an essential activity. The Danish room is shorter and squared, and the camera is facing the meeting table in the middle. The Danish participants are standing behind the chairs of the table, thus they are out-of-sight for the camera. The Danish participants step in front of the blue wall into the camera sight when they asking or answering questions. The facilitator moves out of his way. This maneuver changes the global place of the meeting. Firstly, a new participant entered the space, becoming part of the global place, while another one left the global place, but is still present in the local Danish space. However, the facilitator did not totally leave the global place since he kept providing audio remarks such as "yes" and "ok," making it audibly available to the Indian engineers that he was still "present." The facilitator is still part of the global place through sound.

As for the construction of place-based activities in this type of meeting, it is clear that the "sum" of people present in the local space is not fully included in the global place – they are in the space, but only visibly available in at the Danish site. Moreover, the Danish participants are silent, thus their presence in the global place cannot even be mediated by audio. In large meetings with more than 20 participants, most participants are expected to be silent and participate by listing in and only speaking if they have an issue. In contrast, the Indian participants are all included in the global place, even though they are silent as well, because they are visually available. The video in the War Room meetings has an important role of bridging the local spaces and creating the global place. If we take seriously that place is constructed by the tangle of people, activities, and loci [13], then the global place is transformed by both the projection of peoples' images as well as by the audio sounds they may produce. Thus, while the global space – the sum of the two local spaces – includes all people present (Danish and Indian), the collaborative global place only includes all people with "presences" through audio or video. This is not to say that video and audio are the only ways to mediate presence; clearly many technologies have been developed for exactly this purpose [17]. Instead, this insight tells us something about what is required for two geographically distributed spaces to be connected into one globally collaborative place – namely that we need to mediate the presence of all people available in the local spaces so that they become part of the global place.

5.2 Transforming Global Places and Spaces

GlobalEngineering wanted to reconfigure the localities of the War Room meetings while experimenting with the use of artefacts and digital technologies. They set up a new geographical locality at the Danish site, L10, where they had the opportunity to reconfigure and use a bottom-up approach when designing the space for the War Room meetings. They did not change the Indian locality.

Fig. 3. The co-construction of the space L10 and the mirror wall

The major reconfigurations to L10 were that there was no large meeting table, only three chairs placed by the wall. Due to the new locality, they also did no longer have the high-definition video conferencing equipment available. The room was much larger and six War Room posters hang on three of the walls. In the middle of the room, a desk table was located with a laptop, speakers, mobile video camera, and a projector. The connection to India was a combination of Skype and teleconferencing. The setup in L10 was experimental and re-configurable.

We will refer to the design and re-configuration of the L10 location as a socio-technical construction of the global space for collaboration where the engineers configure and reconfigure artefacts within the local spaces co-constructing the global space. What we saw in L10 was that due to the larger room and lack of meeting table, the participants tended to spread around and was hardly ever captured by the web-camera, even though the web-camera was mobile. Participants would take the camera and point it to the poster, and in this way, the poster became more central, but in many cases, participants would forget about how they were captured and transmitted to the remote site. In these situations, the flexibility of the L10 actually made the place-based activities difficult especially at the remote site. The projection of the remote site in L10 was also transformed, since the Skype connection in many cases was captured by a laptop on the table in India and thus showed less of the room and from the perspective of the table, where the high-definition video-equipment was located so it captured more of the room.

The global space is not simply a social construction [12], but a socio-technical construction including the digital connection, the phone-line and network, the walls, and the projection of images. These are all socio-technical relations, and together they form the global space for collaboration. However, it is not until the connection between L10 and the Indian site is up and running, that the people from both Denmark and India are present, and that the War Room meetings are in progress through various collaborative activities that the combination of L10 and the Indian location emerge as one globally collaborative place. This place is a transformation of the global space; however, it is temporal. As soon as the connection between India and Denmark is closed, the global place ceases to exist, and only traces in the form of the mirrored wall and the digital table of yellow stickers attempt to make the connection persistent. This was clear in the incident were the Danish participant tripped over the electrical wire, resulting in a total breakdown of all of the technical equipment. Here the meeting was interrupted – the global place was gone in a second, leaving only two separate local spaces, and only after the technical connection was re-established did the globally collaborative place emerge again.

6 Discussion

By bringing the collaborative plan for organizing the work of the 300 engineers "outside" the computer and visualizing this on the large War Room posters, the engineers, on the one hand, created more complexities for the global collaboration, and, on the other hand, also brought the "spatial aspects" back to the plan. The computerized plan changes the sense of spatial orientation of the plan by distorting a sense of physical space [11]. So, although it might seem strange to go backwards – from the digital globally shared plans to large paper posters with yellow stickers only accessible from particular geographical locations (especially since the participants are globally distributed) – this move actually brings back many of the inherent characteristics of the collaborative practices, such as space, time, bodily presence, and mutual awareness. Transferring the plan "outside" the computer transforms it into a tangible and persistent artefact useful for handling the articulation work involved in engineering. This move, however, produces new challenges related to the geographical distribution of the engineers because the plan "outside" is not globally available, thus the co-construction of the globally collaborative space as an opportunity for place-based activities becomes essential.

Looking at our empirical case, it was clear that the main argument for designing a special location for the War Room activities was specifically to bring out what was already shared within the computerized collaborative planning tool to the real world and to visualize this in the form of the large brown papers with yellow stickers. Earlier studies on the design of CVE technologies tend to apply the spatial metaphor as a process where the bodies of the participants become represented within the virtual environment in the form of avatars, thus the bodily experience is transformed from the "real" world to the "virtual" world [9]. We saw, in our empirical case, exactly the opposite: namely that what was in the "virtual" world was transformed into to the "real" world – the electronic plan was transformed into the War Room poster. To support the collaborative planning practices, the aim was to create an embodied experience between the participants of the tasks and their dependencies in relation to the larger coherent project.

So, the next question is how did the engineers then create the global space for the embodied experiences of the collaborative planning practices? If space is the opportunity and place is the understood reality [6], then let's start by looking at the construction of the space. Understanding space in the context of global interaction, it is clear that physical boundaries – as the demarcations of where the space begins and ends – are inappropriate concepts. Fitzpatrick et al. [11] suggest "centers" as a more appropriate concept, and thinking about the engineers, it is clear that you might be able to conceptualize parts of the collaborative practices as various centers of attention. So, one set of centers could be the different disciplinary departments (electric, pyro, mills, etc.), each with their team of geographically distributed members. In this perspective, the centers are distinctly different but with overlapping interest and dependencies, and we might conceptualize the War Room meetings as the activities where the center of attention changes from the individual disciplinary centers to interdependencies between the centers. Using the center as a concept, we see that the design of the L10 location is actually a process where the engineers are co-constructing a space for interaction between the various centers of attention and that this design is a co-construction of both the technical artefacts and the social methodologies and processes. Based on our observation, the argument is that the conceptualization of changing centers of attention could be the first "step" in the large leap of developing and applying methods for group-to-group interaction [5] and designing technologies supporting global interaction.

The design of the space has to take into account the global aspect of the interaction, and since the plan is outside the shared technology, the engineers have to find other ways of creating the space. Each of the disciplinary departments has a poster of their own, and we saw in the empirical case that the socio-technical construction of the global space included mirroring the absent posters on the white walls within L10. The engineers needed to create the global space as a mixture of the local and global spaces. However, it was only during the global collaborative practices that the globally collaborative space was established – when the digital connection between India and Denmark was initiated – and that the two geographical localities in mind merged into one globally collaborative space. It was only through the digital connections such as cameras, screens, and audio that the global space emerged.

The global space emerges through the enactment of *place-based activities*. When people begin to initiate activities within the geographical localities space, the global space arises. It is only in the enactment of the space that the shared meaning emerges through the interaction between people, activities, and artefacts – or with Harrison and Tatar's concepts, the place is created in the relations between people, event, and loci [13]. We see here that the space is co-constructed as two interdependent socio-technical entities in the cases where the work is organized as a collaborative effort between geographically dispersed participants. Space and place cannot be seen as two distinct features because they perform only in a co-constructed relationship [12]. Space and place are co-constructed in the actual collaborative practices during the processes where the participants interact and enact the artefacts they bring to the engagement, such as documents, posters, or yellow stickers. It was clear in the three examples of the socio-technical setup of the War Room meetings that re-organizing the space transformed the opportunities for understanding the socio-technical structures co-constructing the place. The spatiality emerged through the enactment of the socio-technical setup of the War Room location (the L10 room) in the actual collaborative actions where the War Room became a place. In the empirical case, it was only during the actual War Room meetings that the space and place were transformed into a meaningful relation through the connections between the people, artefacts, and activities. Only when the participants turned on the video and audio links did the global space for collaborative opportunities arise. The global space did not exist prior to the digital connection, and with the digital connection no global place-based activities can emerges. The Danish and Indian engineers became connected, and the artefacts on both sites entered into one coherent globally collaborative place.

The construction and reconfiguring of the actual global space for the War Room meetings transformed based on the engineers' prior experiences and was, in this way, a social activity involving the construction of the "walls" or "boundaries" of the location (both physically and virtually). But it was only in the actual use of the global space that the geographical localities continuously transformed into one globally collaborative space where meaningful place-based events could occur. The centers of attention were connected.

7 Conclusion

This paper shows how geographically dispersed engineers try to create and co-construct technological opportunities (in a broad sense) to re-encounter and re-imagine the shared collaborative work space, which provides us with the unique opportunity to investigate the production of new spatiality and place-making activities. In this paper, it is argued that globally collaborative spaces are socio-technical co-constructions that become transformed into globally collaborative space during the collaborative practices between dispersed participants. However, global spaces are temporal in nature; thus, only traces of the space can persist outside the meeting activities. We conceptualize how place-based activities are crucial to create a global collaborative space. This crucial work of connecting people and artifacts we have labeled relation work elsewhere [18], and we believe that relation work and the conceptualization of global spaces and places provided in this paper together provides insights essential for new technologies supporting War Rooms meetings. For example, new innovative wall-scale technology-mediated workspaces might benefit to focus on global persistence in information still preserving the tangible nature of collaborative artifacts.

Acknowledgement. Thanks to post.doc Lars Rune Christensen and research assistant Carina Rohrbach for participating in the data collection. GIRI, the Global Interaction Research Initiative at the IT-University of Copenhagen (global-interaction.org) supported this research financially.

References

1. Olson, G.M., Olson, J.S.: Distance Matters. Human-Computer Interaction 15, 139–178 (2000)
2. Hinds, P., Mortensen, M.: Understanding Conflict in Geographical Distributed Teams: The Moderating Effects of Shared Identity, Shared Context, and Spontaneous Communication. Organ Scien. 16(3), 290–307 (2005)
3. Boden, A., Nett, B., Wulf, V.: Trust and social capital: Revisiting an offshoring failure story of a small German software company. In: Proc. European Conference Computer Supported Cooperative Work (ECSCW 2009), Vienna, Austria, September 7-11 (2009)
4. Klemmer, S., Everitt, K., Landay, J.: Integrating physical and digital interactions on walls for fluid design collaboration. Human-Computer Interaction 23, 128–213 (2008)

5. Mark, G., Abrams, S., Nassif, N.: Group-to-group distance collaboration: Examining the "Space Between". In: Proceeding of the Eighth European Conference on Computer Supported Cooperative Work, Helsinki, Finland, September 14-18, pp. 99–118 (2003)
6. Harrison, S., Dourish, P.: Replaceing space: The roles of place and space in collaborative systems. In: Proc. Computer Supported Cooperative Work (CSCW), Cambridge, MA, USA (1996)
7. Hertzum, M.: Six Roles of Documents in Professionals' Work. In: Book Six Roles of Documents in Professionals' Work, pp. 41–60. Kluwer Academic Publisher, Dordrecht (1999)
8. Schmidt, K., Bannon, L.: Taking CSCW Seriously: Supporting Articulation Work. Comput. Support Coop. Work 1(1-2), 7–40 (1992)
9. Benford, S., Greenhalgh, C., Rodden, T., Pycock, J.: Collaborative virtual environments. CACM 44(7), 79–85 (2001)
10. Bly, S., Harrison, S., Irwin, S.: Media spaces: Bringing people together in a video, audio, and computing environment. CACM 36(1), 27–47 (1993)
11. Fitzpatrick, G., Kaplan, S., Mansfield, T.: Physical Spaces, Virtual Places and Social Worlds: A study of work in the virtual, pp. 334–343. ACM, New York (1996)
12. Dourish, P.: Place and space ten years on Respaceing place. ACM, New York (2006)
13. Harrison, S., Tatar, D.: Places: People, events, loci - the relations of semantic frames in the construction of place. Comput. Support Coop. Work 17, 97–133 (2008)
14. Bertelsen, O., Bødker, S.: Cooperation in massively distributed information spaces. In: Proc. European Conference on Computer Supported Cooperative Work (ECSCW), Bonn, Germany, September 16-20 (2001)
15. Forsythe, D.: It's just a matter of common sense: Ethnography as Invisible Work. Comput. Support Coop. Work 8, 127–145 (1999)
16. Randall, D., Harper, R., Rouncefield, M.: Fieldwork for design: Theory and practice. Springer, Heidelberg (2007)
17. Prinz, W.: NESSIE: An Awareness Environment for Cooperative Settings. Kluwer Academic Publisher, Dordrecht (1999)
18. Bjørn, P., Christensen, L.R.: Relation work: Creating socio-technical connections in global engineering. In: Proc. European Conference on Computer Supported Cooperative Work (ECSCW). Aarhus University (fortcoming, 2011)

Why Teens Purchase Virtual Products and Services in Social Virtual Worlds?

Matti Mäntymäki

Turku School of Economics, University of Turku, Finland
matti.mantymaki@tse.fi

Abstract. Purchasing virtual products and services in virtual worlds is a rapidly growing form of online consumer behavior, especially among the younger generations. The aim of the paper is to why teens spend real money in virtual goods and services. We investigate the reasons for virtual purchasing behavior in world's most popular social virtual world, Habbo Hotel. Using content analysis, we classify the reasons for purchasing into four higher order gratifications, namely elevated experience, hedonic and social factors as well as functional activities. The results demonstrate that virtual purchasing is a vehicle for enhancing and customizing the valued aspects in the user experience.

Keywords: social virtual worlds, purchasing behavior, uses & gratifications theory, virtual consumer behavior.

1 Introduction

Social virtual worlds (SVWs) are persistent computer-mediated 3D environments, designed for social interaction and entertainment, where the users are represented as avatars [3]. SVWs can be considered to be a sub-category of social networking sites and a subset of virtual worlds (VWs).

Engagement with SVWs is a rapidly increasing phenomenon; the child-focused Club Penguin and Webkinz alone attract millions of young visitors per month. Purchasing behavior in virtual worlds in also an emerging from of online consumer behavior, especially among the younger generations; the sales of virtual items in Habbo Hotel peaked to 4.5 mil EUR in December 2010. From a wider perspective, VWs influence the way individuals spend their free time and interact with other people but have also been claimed to have a profound societal and economic impact [23].

However, a common challenge for VW operators is how to turn the usage into bottom-line profits. The closure of There is a concrete example of the importance of having a sustainable revenue model in the VW business.

SVWs employ avatars and a 3D environment as the navigational mechanism, which enables new forms for self-presentation and synchronous communication with existing friends, but also with other users. From a theoretical perspective, this makes SVWs distinct from e.g. instant messengers [17] and social networking sites [5] an hence an insightful research context for examining forms of user behavior. Moreover, the fact that the users spend considerable sums of money to enhance their experiences calls for a better understanding of purchase behavior within virtual environments [25].

H. Salmela and A. Sell (Eds.): SCIS 2011, LNBIP 86, pp. 29–40, 2011.

This study fills in three gaps in the literature. First, as addressed by Jung & Kang [11] studies investigating SVW participation from a user perspective have thus far remained scant. Second, the current literature offers a limited understanding of the reasons and factors underlying purchasing behavior in virtual worlds. Third, as addressed by Spence [26], the present VW research has been contextually biased towards the adult audience, particularly Second Life, although services for children represent the majority of VWs.

To fill in the gaps in the literature, this study takes a qualitative approach to investigate the reasons for purchasing behavior inside Habbo Hotel and employs the uses & gratifications theory to identify and classify the reasons for virtual purchasing behavior.

2 Social Virtual Worlds and Habbo Hotel

Virtual worlds can be divided into Gaming Virtual Worlds and Social Virtual Worlds [11]. In contrast to GVWs, SVWs do not have explicit narratives or level-ups. Rather, they open up spaces in which the users define the purpose and content of the usage. According to Bell [4] a SVW can be defined as "a synchronous, persistent network of people, represented as avatars, facilitated by networked computers." As such, SVWs can be further characterised as "non-game spaces where games can be part of them but are not the defining characteristic of a virtual world." (Iqbal et al. 2010, 3191). Consequently, in this study, we define SVWs as *persistent, computer-mediated, networked environments; used for various user-determined purposes such as social interaction, where the users are represented as avatars, and games can be part of the environment, but are not constitutive of the user experience.*

While Second Life is probably the most widely discussed platform, at least with respect to the Information Systems community, Habbo Hotel is the world's largest SVW with about ten times the number users as Second Life. Habbo Hotel is specifically targeted at teenagers; it has 15 million active users in 32 country-specific portals. According to Sulake Corporation, the Finnish platform provider, 90 % of the users are aged between 13 and 18.

Habbo Hotel is a virtual environment, which runs in a web browser environment. Upon first joining, a new user needs to create an avatar, which acts as the user's digital representation in the virtual space. This space "resembles a giant contemporary Western indoor space, presented in isometric 'retro style' three-dimensional graphics and populated by blocky avatars, each controlled by a user" [16]. Habbo avatars do not resemble human beings but are more like cartoon figures. The users are anonymous inside Habbo, revealing one's real identity of contact information is prohibited and moderated by the operator.

Unlike with Second Life, Habbo users cannot manipulate their surroundings. Each avatar is provided with a virtual room that one can decorate with various pieces of furniture and invite other users into. Being in a room together, via their avatars the users can text-chat with each other. In addition, Habbo accommodates various non-violent games users are free to play. Certain events, such as celebrity visits are organized on a regular basis and can participate in dress-up and decoration competitions. Habbo users can use real money to purchase virtual items and premium memberships that provides exclusive features, but Habbo does not apply access fees or periodical subscriptions, so use of the platform is free in general. And in contrast to Second Life, Habbo does not facilitate an in-world economy or a currency that could be exchanged to real money. In sum, the activities Habbo users can engage in relate to social interaction with other users, spending time in various ways, decorating and accessorising their rooms and avatars and trading their virtual possessions with other users inside the platform.

Despite its registered user population of 200 million, Habbo has not been researched to an extensive degree. A search for Habbo using the ProQuest and EbscoHost databases, only returned three relevant academic publications. Griffiths and Light [8] have investigated ethical implications of Habbo as a social platform for teenagers, while Lehdonvirta et al. [16] used Habbo as a vehicle to investigate the nature of consumption of virtual goods. Finally, Iqbal et al. [10] have undertaken a small-scale study among children in a Finnish school into the use of virtual world platforms, only one of which was Habbo. In addition to these studies, the drivers from continuous user participation have been examined by e.g. Mäntymäki & Merikivi [18,19] and purchasing as a key user behavior by Mäntymäki and Mäntymäki & Salo [20,21].

3 Virtual Purchasing Behavior

The distinct characteristic of virtual goods and services (virtual items, characters, currencies, premium memberships) is that they do not have a clear atomistic equivalent or component in them [7], and they can only be consumed and have value inside the virtual environment.

Lehdonvirta [15] conceptually identified three classes of virtual item purchase drivers, namely functional drivers (game performance and advanced characters), hedonic (aesthetic appeal) and social drivers (visual appearance and rare collectibles) [15]. Shelton [24] found that motivations for using Second Life correlated with purchasing of both virtual and real-life products. As there are a large number of other users present in SVWs, it seems plausible to assert that consumption is about building identity, experiences and status similar to real-life consumption habits.

In Habbo, users can buy various virtual items and services with Habbo credits. Virtual items can be used to accessorize the avatar, decorate one's virtual room or to be possessed as collectibles. Furthermore, the users can purchase a premium membership that provides exclusive features compared to the standard account which is free of charge.

To be able to purchase items in Habbo, one must possess Habbo credits that in turn can be purchased with real money similarly than e.g. prepaid mobile subscriptions. In addition to money, one needs to have the user account. Thus, using the SVW temporally precedes purchasing and purchasing behavior.

4 Uses and Gratifications Theory

We employ uses & gratifications (U & G) theory as the theoretical foundation to identify the perceived values underlying virtual purchasing and build the research model. U & G is a media use paradigm from mass communications research that focuses on individual use and choice of media [12]. The main purpose of U & G approach is to explain the reasons why people choose a specific communication medium over alternatives and to elucidate the psychological needs that motivate people to use a particular medium.

U & G asserts that media use is goal-directed behavior aiming to full a core set of needs. Thus, rather than providing a set of predefined factors, U & G acknowledges that media usage is mainly determined by the functions it can serve. U & G has been employed to examine the use of internet, social networking sites and online games as well as virtual worlds [5,27,28].

In their study on the use of Second Life, Zhou et al. [28] distinguished between functional, experiential and social values driving the user participation. With functional values Zhou et al. referred to usage driven by instrumental needs, i.e. to achieve or obtain something through the usage. Experiential values on the other hand relate to usage for its own sake e.g. pleasurable experiences and enjoyment derived from the usage. Thus, functional and experiential values can be viewed to reflect the extrinsic and intrinsic types of motivation [6]. Finally, according to Zhou et al. social values in Second Life were obtained from interacting and forming relationship with other users.

In the present study, we do not use any predefined categories but first examine the most eminent reasons for purchasing behaviour in Habbo Hotel and therefore go deeper into the actual gratifications underlying these reasons.

5   Data Collection

The data was collected through an online survey published on the start page of the Finnish Habbo Hotel portal. Among other questions, the respondents were asked to answer the following open-ended question: *why do you purchase Habbo items and/or premium memberships?* Content analysis was used in classifying the responses [14]. The codification of the empirical data was done by quantifying the reasons mentioned by the respondents. Each response was allowed to fall into several themes when applicable. In all, the codification can be classified data rather than theory-driven.

In total, the survey was opened 8928 times. 3265 respondents proceeded to the final page and submitted the survey. This yielded an effective response rate of 36.6 per cent. To offer the reader an overview of the profile of the respondents, the gender and age distributions are presented in Tables 1 and 2.

The majority of the respondents were females demonstrating that Habbo is able to generate content and activities that attract also the female audience. Table 2 illustrates the age of the respondents. As can be seen from Table 2, 12 and 13 are the most common ages among the respondents.

Table 1. Gender distribution of the respondents

Gender	Frequency	Percent
Female	1860	57.0
Male	1347	41.3
Missing	58	1.8
Total	3265	100.0

Table 2. Age distribution of the respondents

Age	Frequency	Percent
Missing	59	1.8
<10	98	3.0
10	260	8.0
11	504	15.4
12	611	18.7
13	600	18.4
14	438	13.4
15	292	8.9
16	154	4.7
17	71	2.2
18	68	2.1
>19	110	3.4
Total	3265	100.0

From the total pool of responses, a subsample of 1000 respondents was selected to be included in the content analysis. After coding the responses based on the reasons mentioned, the analysis continued with counting the frequencies of different themes mentioned in the responses. As can be seen from Figure 1 presented below, the benefits from having a premium membership, Habbo Club was the most frequently mentioned reason for purchasing in Habbo. The second in terms of frequency was the fun, enjoyment or liking resulting from purchasing in Habbo. The third most frequently mentioned reason was decorating one's virtual room, i.e. the Habbo Home. The fourth theme, labeled as 'Status and self-expression' captured the status as well as self-expression and differentiation from other users via possessing virtual items and/or the premium membership.

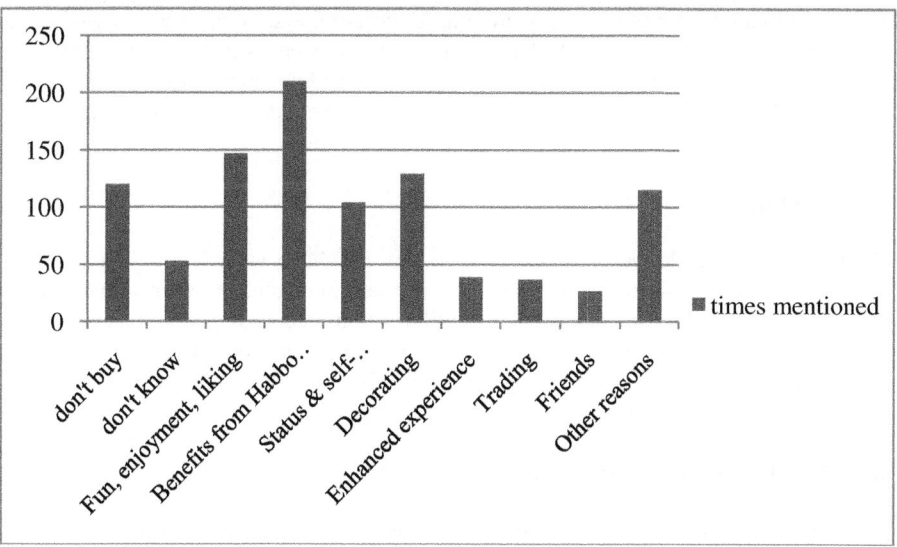

Fig. 1. The most common reasons for purchasing in Habbo Hotel

In addition to this top four, enhanced experience resulting from purchasing, obtaining more friends and trading were frequently mentioned. The category 'other' includes a wide range of less frequently mentioned reasons such as cyber-bullying and escapism. Moreover, a significant degree of the respondents explicitly addressed that they do not spend real money in their Habbo experience. Finally, many respondents were unable to articulate any reason for their purchasing behavior.

6 Gratifications from Virtual Purchasing in Habbo Hotel

6.1 Benefits from the Premium Membership

Having the premium membership provides exclusive features and benefits that are not available for the standard members such as special clothes, hairstyles and accessories as well as an extended maximum number of friends. The benefits from the premium membership are a means for obtaining something else than a goal itself. The value-added from Habbo Club can relate to enhanced status from being recognized as a club member, the wider selection of clothes and accessories as well as additional alternatives related to decorating one's room. Thus, the actual value of Habbo Club depends on the features the user appreciates the most and can be a combination of many factors that then relate to e.g. status, enjoyment, decorating or enhancing the overall user experience.

6.2 Decoration

Decorating one's virtual space i.e. room in Habbo was frequently mentioned as a reason for purchasing virtual items or the premium membership in Habbo. For decoration purposes, the premium membership offers exclusive room designs as well as complimentary furniture every month. Decorating the room was viewed as an entertaining activity per se but also a way to express one's personality or status in Habbo's social scene. Finally some respondents viewed decorating important to create a nice and aesthetic environment to which invite friends or organize parties and games.

6.3 Trading

Some respondents deliberately stated that they purchase virtual items to be traded with other users. This indicates that for the ones interested, trading constitutes an important part of the user experience. Similarly than decorating, trading was viewed both instrumental and a goal itself. Some respondents reported that they trade virtual items to 'become rich' in the virtual world whereas others viewed trading as an entertaining or exciting activity.

6.4 Fun, Enjoyment and Liking

The enjoyment and fun experienced via virtual purchasing were often mentioned as the motives behind purchasing in Habbo. Some respondents reported having developed an affective relationship i.e. liking towards the items they have purchased and possessed. As an example, collectable items tend to have more emotional value that the 'regular' Habbo products. In addition to the enjoyment and personal liking, many respondents viewed purchasing as a mean to boost the enjoyment from Habbo.

6.5 Status and Self-expression

Having the premium membership and/or virtual possession was viewed as a status symbol and consequently, purchasing them as a vehicle for elevating one's status and gaining respect from other users. In addition to merely increasing one's status, virtual purchasing was used to differentiate from others, especially to make a distinction between the 'regular' users and the holders of the premium membership.

An interesting finding related to the status was that many respondents stated that users without the premium membership are discriminated in the social setting and purchasing the Habbo Club account can for some user be more a way to avoid discrimination than enhancing status. To sum up, virtual purchasing can be viewed rather as a vehicle for adjusting one's position in Habbo's social setting rather than simplistically enhancing status.

6.6 Enhanced User Experience

Purchasing was also viewed as a mechanism for making Habbo better in more general terms. Some respondents viewed this in a way that without purchasing the premium membership or virtual items the users experience is not good enough. The distinction between e.g. increased enjoyment or status is that the respondents did not specifically articulate the way purchasing enhances the experience, or focused on the overall experience.

6.7 Friends

Obtaining more friends was viewed as a reason for purchasing. The respondents reported that 'rich' users and Habbo Club members were viewed more popular than the regular users. Thus, status is may be at least partially related to one's social circle. Additionally, as an exclusive feature for the premium members, Habbo Club offers a more extensive 'friend list' i.e. allows the user to accept more people in his social circle as friends. Thus, especially people with extensive social network inside Habbo benefit from the premium membership, which then potentially further reinforces their popularity.

6.8 Other Reasons

The responses categorized under the theme 'other reasons' reflect the variety of motives for using Habbo as well as experiences derived from the usage. As a social virtual world, Habbo does not have narratives or goals, the user determine the actual purpose for their usage. Furthermore, as Habbo is targeted to basically all teenagers, the users are likely to be a heterogenic group in terms of their sociographic background and situations in real life. In sum, the wide range of different other factors driving purchasing was largely expected.

6.9 Classifying the Drivers of Purchasing

Looking the findings through to the U & G lens we have divided the gratifications into four categories, labeled as elevated experience, hedonic factors, social factors and functional activities. Benefits from the premium membership and enhanced experience have been classified to fall into the elevated experience category whereas the hedonic factors category consists of enjoyment. The third category of gratifications was formed to capture the various social factors e.g. status, self-expression and making friends. The third category is formed of functional activities such as decorating one's room and trading virtual items with other users. Table 3 summarizes the categorization of the gratifications.

Table 3. Classification of the gratifications from virtual purchasing behavior in Habbo Hotel

Gratification	Theme	Quotation
Elevated experience	Benefits of the premium membership	"as a member you get access to interesting places" "to get the benefits from the Club memberships. "because with them you get more friends" "then you can have more people as your friends"
	Enhanced experience	"Because it makes visiting Habbo and doing things there better" "…without stuff Habbo would be boring"
Hedonic factors	Enjoyment	"…then it is more fun to be in Habbo" "because of the fun of it" "…then everyone is having fun"
Social factors	Status	"they help to enhance status" "I want to be popular" "to gain respect"
	Self-expression	"to make my group noticed" "…you can better express yourself with clothing" "because the basic clothing does not tell much about one's personality"
	Making friends & socializing	"with stuff you can decorate your own room where you can chat and make friends" "…then it is nice to be in your room and spend time and chat with your friends" "Then you have more friends and you feel more like belong to the group."
Functional activities	Decoration	"to decorate my room" "to make my room more comfortable"
	Trading	"to trade them with others" "to have something to trade"

7 Discussion

7.1 Theoretical Implications

The present study offers new insight on the virtual consumer behavior. The findings demonstrate that the fundamental reasons for virtual purchasing relate to enhancing and customizing the user experience. In other words, virtual items are not purchased to obtain something entirely new but to make the valued aspects in the existing user experience even better. Since SVWs do not have narratives but the users have a large freedom to determine how they want to use the system, Habbo can be considered a type of multi-purpose information systems [9].

Habbo is designed especially for being a recreational environment for teens. Compared to Second Life, Habbo does not facilitate an in-world economy or educational institutions. Hence, the value of Habbo is likely to be related to hedonic and social rather than conventional utility. The central role of hedonic motives i.e. perceived enjoyment in driving sustained the sustained usage of Habbo has also been reported in prior literature [18,19,21,22]. Hence, compared to Zhou et al. [28] who distinguished between functional, experiential and social value from Second Life usage, the gratifications related to purchasing behavior in Habbo concentrate more on experiential and social than functional factors. Nevertheless, congruent with U & G, the results verified that purchasing behavior in Habbo is indeed goal-driven behavior.

The findings clearly reveal the existence of social hierarchies among users and their avatars and demonstrate how virtual purchasing is used to position oneself in the social setting and build virtual self-identity. However, as the users are not allowed to use their real names or reveal their identities inside Habbo, the status and prestige inside the virtual world do not fully transfer to 'real' world and vice versa.

Yet U & G has certain value in categorizing the reasons for virtual purchasing, there is there is a certain overlap between the three broad classes of gratifications that is described in the following quotation:
"because it's so much fun, UC (you see) I like to trade stuff with others and people think you are more cool".

From a theoretical perspective, the overlap can be explained by what Griffiths & Light [8] meant Habbo being an example of convergence of social networking and digital gaming. This study takes the convergence perspective a step ahead by illustrating how profoundly the entertainment value of the SVW is dependent on the presence of other users and how e.g. trading virtual possession or becoming "rich" inside the virtual or other instrumental reasons can the ones that actually drive the experiential gratifications.

7.2 Implications for Business

Given that differentiating from "ordinary" users, gaining status and the exclusive benefits of the premium membership. This indicates that the service operator has been able to find to provide value-added that the users are willing to pay for. At the same time, however, the ordinary users i.e. the ones who do not pay money for the SVW usage are important for the premium users

Furthermore, the user experience should be attractive also without an immediate need for investing money. If the users without the premium membership or purchased virtual possessions start to feel like 'second class' users, they are likely to discontinue using the SVW. Furthermore, signaling status through the premium memberships and owning virtual items is more meaningful when there is a large number of people engaged in the platform. Several respondents described how the premium members are respected more but also how the premium members discriminate the ordinary users. *"Because without them (virtual items) Habbo would be nothing"*, *"because so called 'average joes and janes' are being discriminated"*, *"other people respect you more when you belong to Habbo club, ordinary user are discriminated"*, *"because the others do not want to be friends with you unless you are a Habbo Club member or rich (own lots of virtual items)"*.

These negative incentives may possess a risk for Habbo in the future if they alienate the regular users and give them an impression that all the fun inside the SVW is for the 'insiders'. Selling the premium accounts and value-added services requires that the basic service is able to attract and retain an extensive set of users of whom some can be converted into customers who invest real money in their usage. The success of this business model is hence dependent on retaining the basic users active. As a result, the operators need to carefully balance the benefits gained though purchasing while maintaining the service attractive also the ones who either can or do not want to invest money in their usage

7.3 Limitations and Future Research Avenues

In the present study, we focused on the users of the Finnish Habbo portal. Thus, as a first area of further research additional studies should examine to what extent the findings hold in other context, including the national culture but also the culture of the Habbo portal. In a similar vein, replicating the study in another Habbo portal and/or in another SVW would provide information about the purchasing behavior in other VW platforms.

Second, given the fact that in Habbo social networking and gaming converge, also the reasons for participation and consequently purchasing are various and highly interrelated, as the results of this study illustrate. Hence, to better understand the user's motivation a hierarchical approach to investigate the reasons could be appropriate to understand the mutual relationships and the importance of different motivational factors. Additionally, scrutinizing the relationships and hierarchies between the motivations would also help to better understand the very existence of SVW, i.e. are they in essence social, hedonic or functional platforms.

Third, an important further research avenue would be to examine e.g. psychological, contextual and situational triggers of purchasing behavior in the SVW setting. From a psychological standpoint, understanding how behavioral intentions become activated has been addressed to be a central shortcoming of many prominent theories within social psychology [1,2]. Understanding the factors that act as triggers virtual purchasing would thence be theoretically insightful but also managerially highly relevant.

Fourth, as argued earlier, purchasing can be viewed as subsequent step following continuous usage in the SVW customer relationship. However, there is likely a reciprocal loop between continuous usage and purchasing since the financial commitment in the SVW experience is likely to further reinforce the willingness to participate in the SVW to materialize the returns on the investment. As a result, further research examining the mutual relationships between participation and purchasing behavior and their development would be highly appropriate.

Fifth and finally, active participation in SVWs includes more behaviors than the usage and purchasing. As an example, the Habbo uses and act as tutors for novices, contribute to the various Habbo fansites and share their experiences in social media. Thus, the argument Kim & Son [13] that the post-adoption behavior should be viewed more broadly encompassing other behaviors than usage is very valid also with research on SVW.

References

1. Bagozzi, R.P.: The legacy of the technology acceptance model and a proposal for a paradigm shift. Journal of the Association for Information Systems 8(4), 244–254 (2007)
2. Bagozzi, R.P., Dholakia, U.M.: Antecedents and purchase consequences of customer participation in small group brand communities. International Journal of Research in Marketing 23(1), 45–61 (2006)
3. Bartle, R.A.: Designing virtual words. New Riders, Indianapolis (2003)
4. Bell, M.W.: Toward a definition of "virtual worlds". Journal of Virtual Worlds Research 1(1) (2008)
5. Cheung, C.M.K., Chiu, P., Lee, M.K.O.: Online social networks: Why do students use facebook? Computers in Human Behavior (in Press, Corrected Proof)
6. Davis, F.D., Bagozzi, R.P., Warshaw, P.R.: Extrinsic and intrinsic motivation to use computers in workplace. Journal of Applied Social Psychology 22(14), 1111–1132 (1992)
7. Fairfield, J.: Virtual property. Boston University Law Review 85, 1047–1102 (2005)
8. Griffiths, M., Light, B.: Social networking and digital gaming media convergence: Classification and its consequences for appropriation. Information Systems Frontiers 10(4), 447–459 (2008)
9. Hong, S., Tam, K.Y.: Understanding the adoption of multipurpose information appliances: The case of mobile data services. Information Systems Research 17(2), 162–179 (2006)
10. Iqbal, A., Kankaanranta, M., Neittaanmäki, P.: Experiences and motivations of the young for participation in virtual worlds. Procedia - Social and Behavioral Sciences 2(2), 3190–3197 (2010)
11. Jung, Y., Kang, H.: User goals in social virtual worlds: A means-end chain approach. Computers in Human Behavior 26(2), 218–225 (2010)
12. Katz, E., Blumler, J.G., Gurevitch, M.: Utilization of mass communication by the individual. In: Blumlerand, J.G., Katz, E. (eds.) The Use of Mass Communications: Current Perspectives on Gratifications Research. Sage, Berverly Hills (1974)
13. Kim, S.S., Son, J.: Out of dedication or constraint? a dual model of post-adoption phenomena and its empirical test in the context of online services. MIS Quarterly 33(1), 49–70 (2009)
14. Krippendoff, K.: Content analysis: An introduction to its methodology, 2nd edn. Sage, Thousand Oaks (2004)
15. Lehdonvirta, V.: Virtual item sales as a revenue model: Identifying attributes that drive purchase decisions. Electronic Commerce Research 9(1-2), 97–113 (2009)
16. Lehdonvirta, V., Wilska, T., Johnson, M.: Virtual consumerism. Information, Communication & Society 12(7), 1059–1079 (2009)
17. Li, D., Chau, P.Y.K., Van Slyke, C.: A comparative study of individual acceptance of instant messaging in the US and china: A structural equation modeling approach. Communications of the Association for Information Systems 26(5) (2010)
18. Mäntymäki, M., Merikivi, J.: Uncovering the motives for the continuous use of social virtual worlds. In: Proceedings of the 18th European Conference of Information Systems (ECIS 2010), Pretoria, South Africa (2010)

19. Mäntymäki, M., Merikivi, J.: Investigating the drivers of the continuous use of social virtual worlds, Koloa, Kauai, Hawaii (2010)
20. Mäntymäki, M., Salo, J.: Trust, social presence and customer loyalty in social virtual worlds. In: 23rd Bled eConference eTrust: Implications for the Individual. Enterprises and Society, Bled (2010)
21. Mäntymäki, M.: Customer loyalty in social virtual worlds. Paper Presented at the Proceedings of the 22nd Bled eConference eEnablement: Facilitating an Open. Effective and Representative eSociety, Bled (2009)
22. Merikivi, J., Mäntymäki, M.: Explaining the continuous use of social virtual worlds: An applied theory of planned behavior approach. In: Proceedings of the 42nd Hawaii Conference on System Sciences, Waikoloa, Big Island, Hawaii (2009)
23. Messinger, P.R., Stroulia, E., Lyons, K., Bone, M., Niu, R.H., Smirnov, K.: Virtual worlds — past, present, and future: New directions in social computing. Decision Support Systems 47(3), 204–228 (2009)
24. Shelton, A.K.: Defining the lines between virtual and real world purchases: Second life sells, but who's buying? Computers in Human Behavior 26(6), 1223–1227 (2010)
25. Shin, D.H.: Understanding purchasing behaviors in a virtual economy: Consumer behavior involving virtual currency in web 2.0 communities. Interacting with Computers 20(4-5), 433–446 (2008)
26. Spence, J.: Demographics of virtual worlds. Journal of Virtual Worlds Research 1(2) (2008)
27. Wu, J., Wang, S., Tsai, H.: Falling in love with online games: The uses and gratifications perspective. Computers in Human Behavior 26(6), 1862–1871 (2010)
28. Zhou, Z., Jin, X., Vogel, D.R., Fang, Y., Chen, X.: Individual motivations and demographic differences in social virtual world uses: An exploratory investigation in second life. International Journal of Information Management (forthcoming) (in Press, Corrected Proof)

Difficulties in Establishing Local Language in Machine-Translated Mediated Communication

Mika Yasuoka[1,2] and Pernille Bjørn[2]

[1] Department of Social Informatics, Kyoto University Yoshida Honmachi,
606-8501, Kyoto, Japan
[2] IT University of Copenhagen, Rued Langgaards Vej 7, 2300 Copenhagen S, Denmark
{myj,pbra}@itu.dk

Abstract. Establishing common ground is critical in intercultural communication. Still, little is known as for the practice of common ground in machine-translation mediated communication. In this paper, we report some of the critical communication difficulties related to common ground when intercultural communication is mediated by multilingual collaboration systems. Based on empirical investigation of the communication between Japanese and Danish students applying a multilingual communication system, we identify two main challenges influencing common ground: 1) Difficulties in exchanging socio-emotional aspects and 2) Difficulties in developing shared concepts. As theoretical constructs, social context and project jargon, which are known as essential contributors to the construction and the maintenance of common ground, are harnessed to explain such difficulties.

Keywords: Computer supported intercultural collaboration, multilingual communication, machine translation (MT), shared meaning context, common ground.

1 Introduction

Competences in intercultural communication are vital in our globalized world, and we must be able to collaborate across time, geography, and language boundaries. Among all, language could be one of the most complicated challenges. First, intercultural communication at present has often been conducted utilizing a single standard language (in many cases, English), however, language remains the biggest challenge in some cases. For, many prefer using native language if possible in spite of their decent English literacy [6, 25]. The lack of common language in intercultural settings generates critical challenges for collaborative practices.

Lately, an increasing number of international organizations and multilingual communities have applied support systems for their intercultural communication. One of such multilingual communication support systems is the Language Grid [13], which provides language support at different levels to various settings such as education, medical service, public city service, and NPO activities. The software based on the Language Grid framework, *the Language Grid Toolbox*, provides the bases for our experiment reported upon in this paper.

H. Salmela and A. Sell (Eds.): SCIS 2011, LNBIP 86, pp. 41–55, 2011.
© Springer-Verlag Berlin Heidelberg 2011

In spite of growing demands and use of cutting edge technology to facilitate the interaction in multilingual communication practices, little is known about the impact of current machine translation (MT) on communication in use. It seems clear communication mediated by MT have extra communicational challenges caused by typographical mistakes [6], breakdowns [18], accidental communication halts [27], and inconsistencies and asymmetries of references in pre and post translation [25].

So, what do such challenges mean in intercultural communicative process and how do they influence especially in constructing and maintaining common ground among collaborators? By focusing on locally shared languages, this paper points out participants face further critical difficulties in creating, establishing and maintaining common ground. In order to get preliminary understanding, we conducted a semi-structured empirical experiment of machine-translated intercultural communication by applying the Language Grid Toolbox into the communicative interaction practices of students in Denmark and Japan. Based on the empirical analysis, we found two main challenges in relation to the creation, establishment and maintenance of common ground. They are 1) difficulties in exchanging socio-emotional aspects and 2) difficulties in developing shared concepts. Both challenges influence the possibilities for constructing common ground.

In the remainder of this paper, we first draw our theoretical framework, and then introduce the multilingual collaboration system the Language Grid Toolbox. This is followed by a description of the experiment. We then present our analysis of the experiment explaining the two main findings. Finally, we conclude with a discussion and design implications raised by our study.

2 Theoretical Framework

As theoretical bases, we apply two core concepts, which are common ground and project jargon.

2.1 Common Ground in Intercultural Collaboration

Common ground is defined as language, beliefs, and knowledge that people share for successful collaboration [19]. Common ground exists in situations where the participants are aware that they have information in common [5]. When people collaborate over geographical and national borders, communication breakdowns occur at different levels of social context of the participants as critical challenges [3, 7, 16]. Common ground has originally been discussed in face-to-face conversational context and found it important to meet several conditions related to face-to-face conversation[1]. Later, it is argued common ground could exist by using artifacts [14, 15] including computational artifacts [2, 19] in the geographically distributed settings as well.

---

[1] Such conditions are 1. face-to-face conversation, 2. same physical environment, 3. visibility of each other, 4. speech usage, and 5. simultaneous communication.

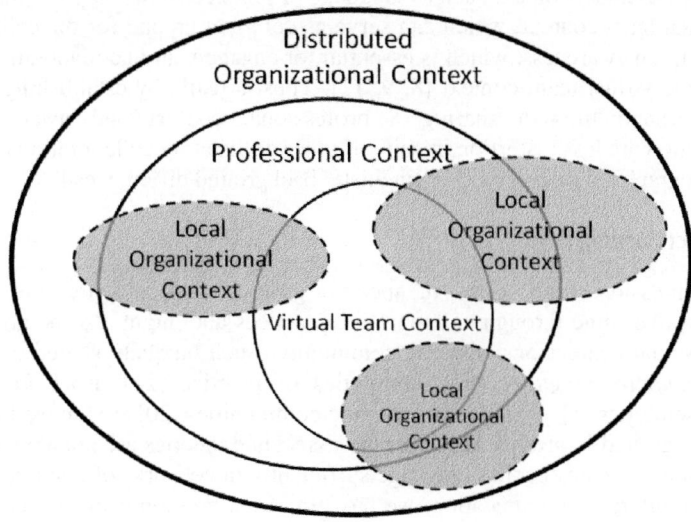

Fig. 1. Shared meaning context, adapted from Bjørn and Ngwenyama [3]

Fig.1 adapted from Bjørn and Ngwenyama [3] illustrates essentials in investigating communication of virtual teams. *The professional context* comprises the language, norms, knowledge, and beliefs that are related to the professional shared activities within the team, e.g. in groups of CS students the professional context might include the common language of software development processes. *The local organizational contexts* are multiple, since each participant brings his or hers local context in to the collaboration. The local organizational contexts of students might include the fellow co-located students, the physical location of the university, and the organizational structures of their education. Initially, *the virtual team context* does not exist. Instead it is initiated at the very beginning of the collaboration, where the participants use time and effort to establish the social context, which then include establishing common ground and communication norm. They may serve as ground for the collaborative activity. *The distributed organizational context* can be seen in large global organizations, which have a high-level of shared norms, organizational language, knowledge, and beliefs across all local contexts, thus affecting both the professional and virtual team context. In educational settings, this could be visible in well-established collaborations between different universities based upon shared goals and hopes for the collaboration.

Professionals engaged in intercultural communication can be analytically delineated into distinct different contexts with a different professional context and in a particular distributed organizational context, all of which influence the virtual team context.

Previous studies have found that successful communication is more evident in cases where virtual team members belong to the same professional domain such as computer engineering or architecture [2, 27]. This shows that sharing common ground based on professional context such as language or practice, would support the creation of the virtual team context, which can serve as common ground for the collaboration over time. Even awareness, which is essential for engagement in collaboration, can be shared in the virtual team context [8, 9, 11]. Thus, a team, by establishing a certain common ground through sharing a professional context and awareness, can communicate with less distortion in spite of other devastating collaboration conditions such as geographical distance [2] or linguistic background differences [19].

2.2 Project Jargon

Words, expressions, and terms in specific groups of people are often socially constructed over time through collaborative practices and might also be grounded in the professional context or a specific community. Such uniquely shared expressions called *community language* in communities of practice [24], *work language* in computer semiotics [1], or jargon in semantic communities [20] are known to function as common ground in groups. However the associated theories are not able to explain characteristics of team specific language sufficiently in networks of community [4] in which intercultural communication, we have in mind, are dominant. Especially how such language are emerged, constructed and shared in local and temporary aligned practice [27] are not articulated.

To serve our objective, we apply the term *jargon* [20, 27]. Jargon is defined as characteristic language such as technical terminology or idiom of a special activity or particular group. According to Robinson [20], in situations where several groups have different practices, traditions, and working objectives, the difficulties emerge because they communicate differently in *jargon*.

Locally used jargon in intercultural communication could be professional expressions acquired through professional education or fostered through professional experience in practice. Such jargon could become *project jargon* which has a high contribution in creating, developing and maintaining common ground to a large extent as things already shared [27]. On the other hand, communication without sharing jargon prevents collaborators largely from having common ground even if they speak common language (such as English) [20, 22].

Project jargon is essential in multilingual communication mediated by MT applications. For example, the Intercultural Collaboration Experiment [18, 27] shows that applying MT to mediate collaboration was successful in spite of all language related difficulties as collaborators shared local jargon based on professional context such as computer science expressions [18, 27]. The experiment also reported on how collaborative repair activities as well as self-repair activities contributed to the creation of project jargon. In self-repair activities, participants improved translation quality through iterative try and error interactions with the MT application. Successful self-repair activities were shared with other team members also improving the general use of the translation tool. In collaborative repair activities, collaborators refined project jargon through interaction with other members and confirmed meanings through interaction processes [26].

The studies mentioned above indicate that project jargon is not only critical for intercultural collaboration but also possible to be created through MT mediated communication. The studies implicate that it might take time. However, created project jargon will play a beneficial facilitation role as common ground.

3 System

The system used in the experiment is the Bulletin Board System (BBS) function of sthe Language Grid Toolbox. The Language Grid Toolbox (the Toolbox) is open source software developed as one of the multilingual collaboration tools of the National Institute of Communication Technologies (NICT), the Language Grid project [13, 17]. Any groups aspiring at establishing intercultural communication could make an agreement with NICT and download the software.

Originally, the Language Grid project was initiated as a reaction to the current situation in language services. Briefly described, it challenges usability and flexibility to add new words, customize domain specific expressions or sentences or combine several services, which current language services lack. The Language Grid is developed as a multilingual service infrastructure, which connect several existing MTs, bilingual corpora, online dictionaries as well as local language services as atomic components and offer cross-language services.

Among several collaboration tools developed based on the Language Grid infrastructure, the Toolbox (See Fig.2) offers a unique interface and improved usability. Its design meets varied needs of multilingual communities with easy function to use. In our experiment, we used only BBS functions for chat in multiple languages. In addition to the functions we use in our study, the Language Grid Toolbox can offer, for example, a distinctive local dictionary function where users can create, develop and maintain a local dictionary. By doing so, the user can combine existing MT functionalities and their local jargon dictionaries.

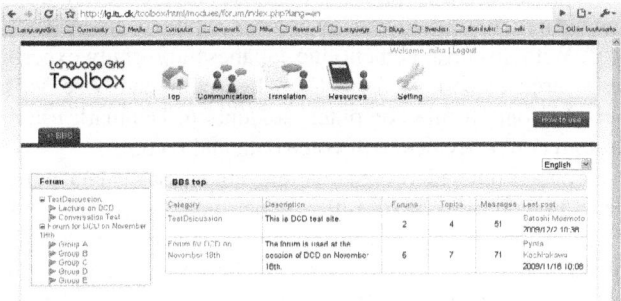

Fig. 2. Language Grid Tool Box and BBS function

4 Setting and Methods

The experiment was conducted as a part of the master course, *Distributed Collaboration and Development* (DCD) at IT University of Copenhagen, Denmark. Participants were nine students located in Copenhagen, Denmark and five students located in Kyoto, Japan. The core analysis targets were students in Denmark while students in Japan took the roles of conversation partner for reasons articulated below. There were five teams in total. In four teams, two in Denmark and one in Japan formed a team and in the last team one in Denmark and one in Japan formed a pair. None of them knew each other before the study and no students in Denmark were familiar with the applications while students in Japan had been involved in developing the applications.

Fig. 3. The DCD classroom and video settings

The study was a semi-structured empirical experiment with no special task except getting acquainted with each other over a fifteen minutes period. This setting was designed intentionally to match a self-introduction activity, which is the first and most significant communication in conventional distributed collaboration in practice.

Prior to the experiment the Toolbox was prepared for DCD. In addition, video Skype was set up to give additional awareness input to students of both sides as shown in Fig. 3. With this arrangement, the Japanese university experiment room was displayed on a large screen in the DCD classroom and vice versa. During the experiment, in additional to the computer, students in Denmark used the five handy video cameras to record activities with voice data and pictures.

For analysis, data from video cameras and all message data posted on the BBS were collected. In addition, before the experiment, students in Denmark were requested to fill out one page questionnaire, which were used to evaluate students' collaboration readiness and collaboration technology readiness [19]. After the experiment, we also conducted extra reflective session to make sense of Danish students' actions. The collected conversation data were analyzed based on protocol analysis [21] and the other empirical data were analyzed based on Olson's four concepts perspective such as collaboration readiness [19].

In this preliminary experiment design, there were two main concerns. First, familiarity to the system of students in Japan might influence largely on behavior of multilingual communication. Secondly, the limited duration of the experiment requires at least one of the members in each group should hold decent technology readiness. As a consequence, core target for analysis were limited only to students in Denmark as a first stage of the experiments.

4.1 The First Session - Preparation

The experiment consisted of three sessions; preparation, communication, and reflective session. First, we review briefly these three sessions.

In the preparation session, fundamental concepts and functionalities of the Toolbox were introduced to students in Denmark. Here they got accustomed to the system design and several functionalities offered in the Toolbox such as back-translation, creation of language paths by combining multiple language resources, and the creation of local dictionaries [13]. In addition, students in Denmark filled out the questionnaire.

The questionnaires had four main questions: Two questions are to evaluate the collaboration readiness mainly knowledge about Japan and Japanese. The remaining two questions were for technology readiness which is subject to check their familiarity to MT, related multilingual communication systems or the Language Grid Toolbox. These barometers are used to analyze influence on collaboration in distance [19]. In our experiment six out of nine Danish students were familiar with Japan and Japanese culture through their hobbies, and two students have Japanese proficiency with intermediate level. Seven students often use on-line MT and none used the Toolbox before.

4.2 Second Session - Communication

After the preparation session, each group opened a browser and logged on to the browser-based Toolbox established at the DCD local server. Five discussion forums on the BBS of the Toolbox were prepared prior to the experiment. Each group member logged on to a specific discussion forum. They wrote, edited, translated, checked back-translation and finally posted messages, and they also answered others' messages. The duration of communication session was fifteen minutes. We will analyze more details in section 5.

4.3 Third Session – Reflective Session

After communication, a shared reflective session was conducted, concerning about their experiences of applying MT when communicating with Japanese students. The followings are a few initial reflections.

4.3.1 Technology Adaptation
Technology adaptation is known as highly influential in the use of any type of groupware technologies [18, 19]. We had expected that the application and its setting would create initial confusions for the students in Denmark. However, they found or invented ways to communicate even over such a short period. Initially, the students with less experience in MT wrote long sentences. Later, they changed their practice and wrote short sentences since long sentences often take a long time to translate and often the result is incomprehensible. Moreover, students stopped using abbreviation or typical chat expressions such as smiley or *U* instead of *You*. Students learnt such words, expressions, and sentences had high possibilities to result in failure in translation. Students in Japan, on the other hand, have already adopted the mentioned aspects as experienced users.

4.3.2 Synchronous with Asynchronous Timing
Students tried composing different sentences before they submitted a message. When they could not comprehend the back-translation results or when they received any

unidentified errors they would revise the sentence before submitting. For this reason, even though their communication was in synchronous mode, one reply message often occupied several minutes. In the reflective session after the experiment, one student explained,

> It was very important to lean back, be patient, relax and take your time. We know it takes time to compose, translate and check messages.

5   Analysis

Based on the analysis, we found two main challenges when students used the multilingual collaboration system to support intercultural communication. They are difficulties in exchanging socio-emotional aspects and difficulties in developing shared concepts. In this section, we introduce each challenge for relating them to our overall analytical framework in the discussion section.

5.1   Difficulties in Exchanging Socio-emotional Aspects

Difficulties in exchanging socio-emotional aspects are raised because of MT in addition to geographical distance, among which we mainly focus on the former.

In communication mediated by MT, social and emotional aspects are often eliminated, which generate confusions and uncertainty about the person behind the MT. Interestingly, many students mentioned their uneasy feelings not knowing their partner. Exploring this issue further in our data, we found that MT seems to blur the personality of users, thus communication difficulties increased. We found the following social and emotional aspects of personality became opaque due to the MT feature.

- *Gender*: When the experiment was introduced to the students the teachers clearly stated they were to engage with five male CS students from Kyoto University. In addition, the *skype* image of the students in Japan was projected on the wall in front of the students during the whole experiment. Still, they were confused about the gender of their collaborators in Japan. In the reflective session, some students expressed their confusions about the gender of their Japanese partner.
- *Intention:* When people talk face-to-face or even on the phone, explicit or implicit intention is often carried in words, sentences and ways of speaking, which might not be translated by MT easily. Some messages from Japan were difficult to understand in spite of its high translation quality. We do not argue that Japanese students intentionally made their message opaque. Instead, we argue that MT tends to distort the intention behind the utterances, making it more complex for collaborators to make sense of particular utterances.
- *Rich details*: In communicating, rich details often provide better insights as for the matter discussed. However during the experiment students quickly found that they had to write short sentences with simple language structures. At the same time, we observed unintentional elimination of message details processed through MT. This way of communication reduced the rich details within the conversations, making the communication plainer and less engaging.

All socio-emotional aspects including gender, intention, and rich details are typically used in order to make sense of each other during conversations but they were not fully supported by MT. Thus, their communication carried only a limited socio-emotional aspect.

5.2 Difficulties in Developing Shared Concepts

Difficulties in developing shared concepts are raised because of speculations partly caused by MT. We review two aspects focusing on MT influences.

5.2.1 Communication Mediated by Machine Translation

MT concerns how words, expression, and sentences are translated from original *Language A* to targeted *Language B and C*. For MT users, it is usually difficult to evaluate the quality of the translation results without having proficiency of the targeted language. However, the Toolbox provides the possibility for users to verify the translation quality through back-translation features [13]. The users have an opportunity to comprehend how their messages could be conveyed to the partner to some extents.

In communication mediated by MT, the following four types of communication are roughly probable.

- Type 1: Word, expressions, and sentences in Language A is translated into Language B and C correctly, and taken as a correct translation.
- Type 2: Word, expressions, and sentences in Language A is translated into Language B and C wrongly, and taken as a mistranslation.
- Type 3: Word, expressions, and sentences in Language A is translated into Language B and C correctly, but taken as a mistranslation.
- Type 4: Word, expressions, and sentences in Language A is translated into Language B and C wrongly, but taken as correct translation.

The first and second communication types do not generate further issues. However, the third and fourth communication types are rather unique for communication mediated by MT and could lead communication challenges.

5.2.2 Communication with Over-Speculations

Because of the prevailed use of MT nowadays, users often know MT could make mistakes by mistranslating or by misapplying grammatical structures. Consequently, experienced MT users pay attention to how the system might translate from original language to the others. In order to get better translation, users are known to adapt themselves to the system for example by simplifying and shortening their messages to be processed preferably. On the other hand, inexperienced or novel users might not realize how MT makes mistakes, but yet, they can gradually learn and often adjust themselves to the technology [18, 25, 27]. This is also true in our study. Experienced students often manipulated their messages and students with less experience began to learn and modified their writing and editing behavior even in such a short period.

At the same time, experienced users sometimes over-speculate MT results, which cause the third communication type mentioned above. They thought MT mistranslated the message even though it was correct. In our experiment we saw this phenomenon.

F.x. several Japanese students mentioned artificial intelligence and *service computing*[2] as their research topics. Even though service computing is a rather new expression, it is known among CS professionals and gradually recognized in other domains.

Students in Japan were familiar with the expression. When students in Denmark encountered this concept in the translated sentences they thought it as mistranslation since they did not know the term, and the sentence did not make any sense to them.

Table 1. Over-speculation on MT

Japanese Screen	Danish Screen
D: John studies digital design and communication. Michael studies software development and technologies. **J: Wonderful. I study artificial intelligence and *service computing*.**	**D; John is studying digital design and communication. Michael is studying software development and technology.** J: Wonderful. I'm studying artificial intelligence and a *service computing*.

Left column of Table 1 shows how Japanese students saw messages while right column shows how Danish students saw messages. Students in Japan wrote and display messages in Japanese while students in Denmark wrote and display messages in English. (Note that messages of Japanese screen are translated to English by authors for the readers' convenience.) *D* represents messages from Denmark while *J* represents messages from Japan. Original utterances are shown in bold.

As shown in Table 1, the translation of the concept *service computing* from Japanese to English is correct except redundant 'a', which might make the concept unclear to students in Denmark. Not knowing the concept they interpreted it as mistranslation and avoided to ask further questions about the term consciously. In the reflective session the Danish student explained:

> Service computing confused me a lot. Do they study economics? What is it? I know MT mistranslated it. (The organizer explained the meaning) Oh... so, it is a proper noun..., technical term. They should put the term in brackets so that I could ask what it is. (bold by authors)

In this case, the term was translated correctly, but not became project jargon among the team. Instead, they avoided clarifying the meaning. If they had known that 'service computing' was not a wrong translation, they might had engaged themselves more to the communication and become project jargon.

Viewing this observation in respect to the shared meaning context framework (see Fig.1), we can see that the CS student in Japan provides as the concept *service computing*, which is influenced by their professional context (they learnt it during their CS education) as well as their local context (this is a well known term in their research lab). However, they do not manage to transform the concept into a shared concept, namely project jargon within the virtual team context, since the students in Denmark does not understand it. From their perspective, service computing is not part of their professional context, nor part of the local context.

---

[2] An emerging cross discipline, which aims at leveraging low-cost development of distributed applications.

As shown, communication mediated by MT can be easily disrupted in spite of the success translation. This over-speculation of MT, or Type 3 communication, generated a certain difficulties in developing project jargon.

5.2.3 Guessing from the Context

Experienced users of MT over-speculate as well as adjust themselves to MT as shown. However, there are also situations, where the mistranslated concepts did not disturb the conversations, since it was possible for the participants to guess the correct meaning from the particular context of the conversation, namely Type 2 communication. This does not mean that the participants overlooked translation errors, but instead that they were not bothered since the meaning of the sentence could be easily guessed.

In our experiment, some key expressions were mistranslated from the original language to the target languages. For example, the key expression *the Language Grid* was translated as *a linguistic grid* from Japanese to English (see Table 2). In this particular case, it was obvious for students that the 'a linguistic grid' meant 'the Language Grid', because of the particular experiment setting. But if the same translation mistake had happened in a different conversation in a different virtual team context, this might not be the case, in which the translation mistake might disrupt the meaning of the conversation.

Table 2. Guessing from the context during MT

Japanese Screen	Danish Screen
D: ...My specialization is digital design and communication. What is specialization in master class? **J: My specialization is intercultural collaboration using the Language Grid. I used to study communication network.** D: Ok. I am very new in this kind of software. Do you have a lot of experience?	**D:...My specialization is digital design and communication. What is the specialization of your masters degree?** J: My specialty is different culture collaboration using a linguistic grid. (The rest of the sentence was not translated.) **D: Ok. I'm pretty new with this kind of software. Do you have much xperience with it?**

Table 2 shows screen messages. In this case, students in Japan used the term the Language Grid as project jargon in the particular shared virtual team context (see Fig.1). However, the term 'the Language Grid' was translated into 'a linguistic grid'. Due to the translation error, two terms both referring to the same application became a part of the virtual team context, namely 'the Language Grid' equal to 'the linguistic grid', without disrupting the conversation. Thus, consequently both terms existed as a shared concept in virtual team context.

As shown, intercultural communication mediated by MT can be easily disrupted by mistranslation. Nevertheless, this also shows that participants' perception and interpretation of the particular context might support the participants in 'guessing' the true meaning of mistranslations and overcoming translation errors without disruption.

6   Discussion

What are the additional challenges when using MT applications as a mediating technology for communication in an intercultural and geographically distributed team? Investigating communication between students in two locations and languages, we identified two main challenges: difficulties in exchanging socio-emotional aspects and difficulties in developing shared concepts and furthermore project jargon.

6.1   Difficulties in Exchanging Socio-emotional Aspects

This challenge is related to the mediation of social clues which guides the interpretation of others actions and utterances, thus contributes awareness of others' actions and influence collaboration [12]. The social translucence systems approach [10] have exactly been designed to try to bridge this problem of awareness, and translucence in communication structures for virtual teams have been found essential to decrease communication breakdowns. Our data supports this argument. However where social translucence systems more generally relate to all types of collaborative technologies, our study suggests that mediating social clues by creating translucence in communication structures is a highly complicated matter in MT, since the automatic translation and type 3 and 4 communication remove any social signifiers from the utterances.

6.2   Difficulties in Developing Shared Concepts

Establishing common ground is a process of creating a shared meaning context [7, 19] persisting of shared knowledge, contexts, and context dependent jargon [27]. In our experiment it was not the easy task to develop common language as shown in the example of *service computing*. However, we also saw that in some cases even mistranslations can make sense for the participants and they could share concepts, if the context for the conversation can be utilized for guessing the meaning between lines.

Our study shows it is a big challenge to keep consistency pre and post translation from original language to other languages. Correctly translated words were sometimes taken as mistranslation, while mistranslated words sometimes do not bother users. Our preliminary understanding is that it is difficult to create project jargon in intercultural communication, consequently common ground. However, for overcoming the difficulties, our data also revealed potentially beneficial strategies, namely, over-speculating translation results and guessing to avoid disruptions in addition to well known strategies such as adjusting themselves to systems.

7   Conclusion

In this paper, we examined impacts of MT on intercultural communication in distance based on the semi-controlled experiment and its empirical analysis. We highlighted the impacts on common ground in relation to the social context and project jargon. Through the analysis, we identified two challenges, namely the difficulties in exchanging socio-emotional aspects and the difficulties in developing shared concepts.

Exchanging socio-emotional aspects is difficult because language translation prune off details clues of the personalities engaged in the conversations such as gender, intention and other rich details. All these socio-emotional clues are essential for the participants to construct a virtual team context, different from, but based upon, the distributed organizational context each participant is situated within. Developing project jargon is difficult because it is typically done overtime through frequent interaction.

This work has several limitations. The analysis focused on only one side mainly for practical reasons such as limited experiment duration and users' system adaptability, so considerations cannot be generalized for both sides. The experiment durations also affect the development process of project jargon, which might require weeks, months or more. Thus, we speculate that the students, giving more time as well as a clear coupled work task would start to develop and use the local dictionary within the system to construct project jargon supporting common ground. In addition, English was not mother tongue to almost all Danish university students' so we cannot neglect possibilities that some issues might stem from their English proficiency even though they use English as a common language at the university and we did not acknowledge the matter during experiments and analysis.

Nevertheless, the experiment also showed us something unique for MT, namely the participants' ability in actually engaging with others in the multilingual setting, giving the short time span. Moreover our study shows how students could evoke creative minds in order to avoid communication breakdowns by aligning MT technologies. The strategy of over-speculation entails that the user are highly skeptical towards translation results, thus in cases of doubt the participants will ignore the results as mistranslation instead of exploring the unclearness of the results further. In the guessing strategy, students encountering unclear concepts simply guess the meaning of the concept based upon the context without further fuss. We saw that these strategies worked.

In a design perspective these strategies might be a new ground for the design of MT applications, since systems supporting creative guessing might be an alternative than repeatability and grammatical accuracy. Thus, we argue the goal for MT application will be to support establishing project jargon and common ground, and to mediate socio-emotional clues and guessing behavior in which the implicit clue can persist but not simply be lost in translation, rather than seeking for grammatically correct translation.

There is a range of implications to future research. More empirical and semi-structured studies with longer experiment durations will help to understand how four communication types are characterized, how project jargon is established over time and how the shared meaning context is influenced when using MT applications in intercultural communication in distance. Holistic analysis from both locations and multiple languages under similar conditions will clarify the impact of MT as a mediating technology further more.

Acknowledgments. We thank the Language Grid projects for letting us provide the system for our educational use. We also thank master students at Kyoto University and IT University of Copenhagen to join our experiment. This research was partially supported by a Grant-in-Aid for Scientific Research (A) (21240014, 2009-2011) from

Japan Society for the Promotion of Science (JSPS) and Kyoto University Global COE Program: Informatics Education and Research Center for Knowledge-Circulating Society,

References

1. Andersen, P.B.: A Theory of Computer Semiotics. Cambridge University Press, Cambridge (1990)
2. Bjørn, P.: Virtual project teams – distant collaborative practice and groupware adaptation. Ph.D thesis, Roskilde Universitetcenter (2006)
3. Bjørn, P., Ngwenyama, O.: Virtual team collaboration: Building shared meaning, resolving breakdowns and creating translucence. Information Systems Journal 19(3), 227–253 (2009)
4. B.J.S., Duguid, P.: Knowledge and Organization: A Social-Practice Perspective. Organization Science 12(2), 198–213 (2001)
5. Clark, H.: Using language. Cambridge University Press, Cambridge (1996)
6. Climent, S., Moré, J., Oliver, A., Salvatierra, M., Sànchez, I., Taulé, M., Vallmanya, L.: Bilingual newsgroups in Catalonia: A challenge for machine translation. Journal of Computer-Mediated Communication 9(1) (November 2003)
7. Cramton, C.D.: The Mutual knowledge problem and its consequences for dispersed collaboration. Organization Science 12(3), 346–371 (2001)
8. Dourish, P., Bellotti, V.: Awareness and coordination in shared work spaces. In: Proceedings of Computer-Supported Cooperative Work (CSCW), Toronto, Canada, pp. 107–114. ACM Press, New York (1992)
9. Dourish, P., Bly, S.: Portholes: Supporting awareness in a distributed work group. In: Proceedings of Human Factors in Computing Systems (CHI 1992), pp. 542–547. ACM Press, New York (1992)
10. Erickson, T., Kellogg, W.A.: Social translucence: An approach to the designing systems that support social processes. ACM Transactions on Computer-Human Interaction 7(1), 59–83 (2000)
11. Heath, C., Svensson, M.S., Hindmarsh, J., Lulff, P., Lehn, D.: Configuring awareness. Computer Supported Cooperative Work (CSCW) 11(3), 317–347 (2002)
12. Hinds, P., Mortensen, M.: Understanding conflict in geographical distributed teams: The moderating effects of shared identity, shared context, and spontaneous Communication. Organization Science 16(3), 290–307 (2005)
13. Ishida, T.: Language grid: An infrastructure for intercultural collaboration. In: Proceedings of IEEE/IPSJ Symposium on Applications and the Internet (SAINT 2006), pp. 96–100 (2006)
14. Lee, C.P.: Between chaos and routine: Boundary negotiating artifacts in collaboration. In: Proceedings of the 9th European Conference on Computer-Supported Cooperative Work (ECSCW 2005), Paris, pp. 387–406 (2005)
15. Lee, C.P.: Boundary negotiating arifacts: Unbinding the routine of boundary objects and embracing chaos in collaborative work. CSCW 16, 307–339 (2007)
16. Malhotra, A., Majchrzak, A.: Enabling Knowledge Creation in Far-flung teams: Best Practice for IT Support and Knowledge Sharing. Journal of Knowledge Management 8(4), 75–88 (2004)

17. Murakami, Y.: Ishida, & T. Nakaguchi, T. Infrastructure for language service composition. In: Proceedings of the Second International Conference on Semantics, Knowledge, and Grid (SKG 2006), pp. 1–5 (2006)
18. Nomura, S., Ishida, T., Yamashita, N., Yasuoka, M., Funakoshi, K.: Open source software development with your mother language: Intercultural collaboration experiment. In: Proceedings of HCII 2003 (2003)
19. Olson, G.M., Olson, J.S.: Distance matters. Human Computer Interaction 15, 139–178 (2000)
20. Robinson, M., Bannon, L.: Questioning representations. In: Proceedings of the Second European Conference on CSCW 1991, pp. 219–233. Kluwer Academic Press, Dordrecht (1991)
21. Ericsson, K.A., Simon, H.A.: Protocol analysis: Verbal reports as data. MIT Press, Cambridge (1993)
22. Star, S.L.: The cultures of computing. Sociological Review Monograph. Blackwell Publishing, Malden (1995)
23. Takano, Y., Noda, A.: A temporary decline of thinking ability during foreign language processing. Journal of Cross-Cultural Psychology 24, 445–462 (1993)
24. Wenger, E.: Communities of Practice: Learning, Meaning and Identity. Cambridge University Press, Cambridge (1999)
25. Yamashita, N., Ishida, T.: Effects of machine translation on collaborative work. In: Proceedings of the 2006 20th Anniversary Conference on CSCW, pp. 515–524 (2006)
26. Yasuoka, M.: Collaboration support in the initial collaboration phase. In: Proceedings of Participatory Design Conference, vol. 2, pp. 129–132 (2006)
27. Yasuoka, M.: Bridging and Breakdowns – Using computational artifacts across social worlds. Ph.D. thesis, IT University of Copenhagen (2009)

Lazy User Model: Solution Selection and Discussion about Switching Costs

Mikael Collan[1] and Franck Tétard[2]

[1] Pori Unit, University of Turku, School of Economics,
P.O. Box 170, 28101 Pori, Finland
[2] Department of Information Technologies, Åbo Akademi University,
Joukahaisengatan 3-5, 20500 Åbo, Finland
ywmcol@utu.fi, franck.tetard@abo.fi

Abstract. Research on user acceptance and adoption of technology represents an important body of knowledge within the field of information systems. The Lazy User Model has been recently introduced as a new way to understand user acceptance and adoption of technology, when several competing solutions are available. This model asserts that user selection is based on factors such as the identified user need, the user state, and the overall effort related to the use of technology. In this paper, we suggest that a user will most often choose the solution that will fulfill a need with the least effort, discuss the concept of switching costs and learning in connection with technology selection. Lazy User Model seems to capture important elements of solution selection, implying that the model may help in better understanding the factors that determine the success of mobile services

Keywords: user adoption, user selection, switching costs, learning.

1 Introduction

User adoption and acceptance of technology and attachment to devices and services has been studied with a number of models like the Technology Acceptance Model (TAM) [1, 2], Unified Theory of Acceptance and Use of Technology (UTAUT) [3], Technology Task Fit (TTF) [4, 5], and HCI aspects with, e.g., cognitive fit theory [6, 7]. To our knowledge there are, however few theories that try to explain how users select devices or services, when there are numerous possible solutions. Lazy User Model (LUM) is a theory that explains the user solution selection process that demands the *least effort*.

Ideas regarding the use of least effort or least energy to fulfill a need can be found in physics (e.g. water flowing downhill follows the *path of least resistance*), but similar ideas have also been presented in behavioral sciences, e.g., in linguistics to explain scaling of human language [8, 9], where Zipf called his theory the *principle of least effort*. In information seeking (informatics) the theory of least effort was picked by Mann [10] as one of the principles guiding information-seeking behavior and hence the design of modern libraries.

H. Salmela and A. Sell (Eds.): SCIS 2011, LNBIP 86, pp. 56–68, 2011.

The term *"lazy user"* has been used previously, e.g., in information seeking (text retrieval) [11], (user that uses only limited effort), in context aware computing [12] (user that demands the best effort – result trade-off), and in interactive feature selection [13] (sloppy user that is not precise in her selection).

Some similar issues are also researched in finance, e.g., "lazy banking" [14] is research into how banks are not willing to invest efforts into turning around failing businesses, but prefer to liquidate, because liquidation is the *least costly* and the most certain alternative. It is interesting to note that in corporate finance effort can usually be measured with monetary units.

The objectives of the paper are twofold: (i) to present the Lazy User Model and to compare it to other established models and theories in the field of user acceptance and adoption of technology, and (ii) to discuss how the Lazy User Model can be used to understand switching costs (in changing technologies) and the importance of usability and learning.

In the next section we give a short literature review of technology adoption models and related research. In the third section, we present the Lazy User Model and compare it with existing literature and models. In the fourth section we discuss switching costs and learning costs and how these can be modeled and understood within the Lazy User Model framework. In the fifth section, we discuss implications of the theory on the design of products & services. We close with a summary and discussion.

2 User Acceptance and Adoption of Technology – Literature Review and Related Research

Technology adoption models and user acceptance of technology have been the subject of extensive research within the information systems (IS) community. In our literature review, we identify several models and theories explaining technology adoption. These theories and models aim at identifying the factors that favour technology adoption. In the following sub-sections, we will review several theories of technology adoption; the purpose is not to criticize these models, but to analyse them in order to understand how our model relates to these established theories.

2.1 Theory of Reasoned Action (TRA)

TRA originates from social psychology. The model is based on three constructs: behavioral intention, attitude (beliefs about the consequences of adopting a behavior) and subjective norm ("the person's perception that most people who are important to him or think he should or should not perform the behavior in question" in Fishbein and Azjen [15]. The model suggests that behavioral intention is dependent on the attitude about the behavior and the subjective norm. The model has been criticized for its limitations where one has to make a choice between several alternatives (see [16] p. 325).

2.2 Technology Adoption Model

The technology adoption model (TAM) was originally developed by Davis and Bagozzi [2] TAM is one of the extensions of the theory of reasoned action described earlier. Like TRA, TAM includes behavioral elements, i.e. it assumes that certain variables will directly or indirectly affect the intention to act.

In TAM, the main variables are Perceived Usefulness (PU) - defined as "the degree to which a person believes that using a particular system would enhance his or her job performance", and Perceived Ease-of-Use (PEOU) - defined as "the degree to which a person believes that using a particular system would be free from effort". PU and POU impact on the intention to use, which in turn impacts on actual usage behavior. TAM is one of the most influential adoption models within the IS community. The original study by Davis has been replicated and tested several times. Results have validated the reliability of the model [19], although it has been criticized for its low predictive value. What is also important to remember is that TAM uses user perceptions as variables.

2.3   Unified Theory of Acceptance and Use of Technology (UTAUT)

UTAUT is a model developed by Venkatesh et al. [3]. The model is an effort to consolidate and unify eight earlier models on technology system usage (TRA, TAM, motivational model, theory of planned behavior, a model combining the technology acceptance model and the theory of planned behavior, model of personal computer utilization, innovation diffusion theory, and social cognitive theory). The model uses four key constructs (performance expectancy, social influence, effort expectancy and facilitating conditions) as direct determinants of usage intention. Four key moderators are also identified: gender, age, experience, and voluntariness of use.

2.4   Technology-Task Fit (TTF)

TTF argues that technology is more likely to have a positive impact on individual performance if the technology is aligned with the characteristics of the task(s) that the user has to perform. The model has been developed by Goodhue and Thompson [5]. The theory provides a measure (measure of task-technology fit), which is used as a predictor of improved job performance and effectiveness.

2.5   Diffusion of Innovation

Diffusion is "the process by which an innovation is communicated through certain channels over time among the members of a social system" [17]. The theory is developed by Rogers and explains how and why innovations spread across cultures (organisations, society, communities…). Some of the key constructs used in the Diffusion of Innovation theory are: Relative advantage, Ease of use, Image, Visibility, Compatibility, Results demonstrability, and Voluntariness of use [18]. One limitation of the theory is that all users do not have the same motivations for adopting technology.

2.6   Criticism of Current Research on Technology Adoption

Research on technology adoption is mainly conducted today within the framework of the TAM model, which is the most influential and dominant technology adoption framework. Though TAM research has clearly been able to demonstrate that perceived ease of use (POU) and perceived usefulness (PU) are two important determinants of technology adoption, POU and PU have been largely treated as black boxes [19]. In Benbasat and Barki [19], TAM research is criticized for neglecting to study important behaviors such as reinvention and learning, which are relevant to understanding adoption. They also claim that a deeper understanding of usefulness is needed, but not possible because of the lack of theory of usefulness. They also advocate the need for research that focuses on longitudinal studies that assess system use over time and the interplay between the varieties of behaviors that users engage in, instead of a *"single, narrowly conceptualized usage behavior of past research"*. The LUM model that we present in the next section tackles these shortcomings by introducing the concepts of learning and the dynamic aspects of solution selection.

3 The Lazy User Model

3.1 Background

Lazy user model (LUM) was presented in Collan [20] and was further developed in [21, 22, 23]. The model was developed to place more focus on the user in technology acceptance research. Several prominent theories in acceptance research are mainly focused on technology (e.g., TRA, DOI, TTF). The lazy user model, on the other hand, places focus on the needs and characteristics of the user in the dynamic process of solution selection, when several competing solutions are available. Furthermore, the theory focuses on the effort demanded by the user (user effort), when selecting a solution to a problem from a set of possible solutions. According to the lazy user model, a user is likely to choose the solution that demands the least effort [21, 22].

Unlike most prominent technology acceptance theories, LUM proposes that technology acceptance is impacted by *the principle of least effort*. The principle can be found in various fields of research. In physics the principle is called *the path of least resistance*, and is seen in everyday phenomenon such as electricity or water running down a path of least resistance. Zipf [8] described similar issues when he explained the scaling of human language in *The Principle of Least Effort*. His theory has received support by other researchers, such as Ferrer i Cancho [9], studying Zipf's theory of least effort in the scaling of human language, and Zanette [24] in studying the creation of musical context. The principle of least effort finds support also in results from medical research, which has found evidence for the human brain applying *the law of least effort* when solving a problem Reichle [25].

3.2 The Construct of the Lazy User Model

The goal of lazy user model is to "try to explain how an individual (user) makes her selection of solution to fulfill a need (user need) from a set of possible solutions (that fulfill the need)" [22]. LUM proposes that from a set of possible solutions, which are limited by the circumstances *(user state)*, the user will choose the solution that demands the *least effort* from her in order to fulfill the need. This process is referred to as *solution selection* [22].

A solution selection process is sparked by the need of the user. The **user need** is an "explicitly specifiable want", either tangible or intangible, that can be fulfilled completely. The lazy user model can be applied to situations where a need or problem has several different solutions. Hence, the user need *defines* the set of possible solutions that will solve a problem. The need for information, such as flight timetables, is an example of an intangible need that can be fulfilled completely, by many different solutions; in order to acquire flight timetables one might, e.g., use text-TV, the Internet, ring the airport flight timetables, or send a text message asking for the information. The concept of *user need* applies to any situation where a user has a specific need that can be fulfilled completely by one of several solutions [22].

The **user state** is a description of both the user and the circumstances that surround her at the time of the need. User state includes *characteristics* of the user, such as age, gender, social and cultural belonging and experience, including any type of experience that is relevant for solving or fulfilling the problem or the need in question. The *circumstances* that surround the user at the time of the need may be very specific. The most important circumstances include location, available time and available resources. *Location* refers to, among other, whether the user is inside or outdoors or "on the go" at the time of the need, if the location is familiar or unfamiliar (e.g. at home or in a foreign country), and the time of day (e.g. in the morning the user might be in a hurry to get to work, whereas the evening might be spent comfortably at home); *available time* refers to the amount of time the user can spend; whether a solution to a need or problem is needed within seconds, or whether the user has possibility to wait for days or even weeks; *available resources* refer to the resource options the user has for selecting a solution. Available resources could, for example, include taking the bus, bike, taxi, car, or walk from point A to point B, or paying with cash, a payment card, Internet or the mobile phone. If the user does not have a car or a bike, these options are naturally excluded from the possible solutions. Consequently, user state *limits* the set of possible solutions that fulfill a need or solve a problem [22]. The effects of user need and user state are depicted in an illustration of the lazy user model in figure 1.

The factors describing user state (characteristics and circumstances) are supported by other technology acceptance researchers. Constantinou [26] presents a theory discussing individuals' choice process of advanced mobile data services, stressing the impact of *background context* and *local context* in the user's choice process. The background context refers to the user's previous experience and knowledge about a product or service with similar characteristics. The local context refers to how the user is affected by how a new service or a product and its substitutes are presented. Additionally, the local context refers to the context of use, including "physical location and the availability of substitute products/services" [26]. Other acceptance theories also indirectly consider some characteristics of the user. UTAUT highlights the influence of age, experience and social influence on user acceptance [3]. In the field of marketing, Kotler [27] presented factors influencing buyer behavior, which are very similar to the factors influencing user state. Thus, user state very strongly depicts who the user is, the possibilities and limitations of the user and, therefore, strongly limits the possible solutions at hand.

Considering the flight timetables example, the possible solutions would be limited by the user state. Thus, a user with no access to the Internet would be forced to exclude this option from her list of possible solutions. A mobile phone user sitting on a bus, in urgent need of the timetables, would be forced to exclude most other alternatives than using the mobile phone to acquire the needed information, whether it be to use SMS, the Internet, or phoning someone.

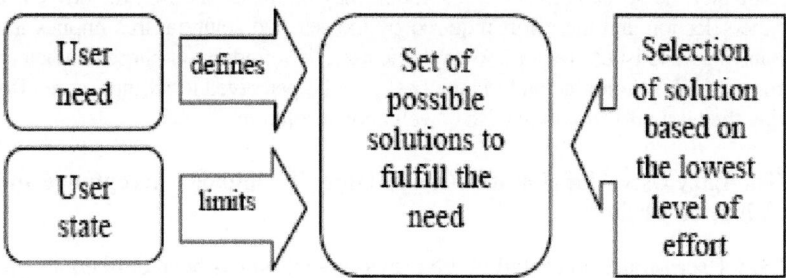

Fig. 1. The lazy user model. The model shows the effect of user need and user state on the available solutions, and the decisive role of perceived effort.

Once the user need and user state have defined and limited the set of possible solutions, the solutions may be delivered by using different products, devices or services. The solution that, according to the model, is selected is the solution that requires the ***least effort*** from the user. Effort, as defined in Tétard et al [22] can be measured in various forms, and is the combination of money spent, time used, and energy used (physical or mental work). The different forms of effort do not necessarily carry equal weight, but may vary from situation to situation and from user to user. Situations requiring a combination of the forms of effort entail an individual estimation and transformation function between the different forms. Regardless of the form of effort used, the less effort overall that is required of the user, the better. Thus, in every different situation a user has to make an individual estimation of the level of effort demanded by different solutions in order to select the solution that demands the least effort [22]. This is in line with a study on human problem solving presented by Newell and Simon [28], who observed that human problem solvers will generally seek ways to reduce their problem solving effort. This mode of thinking has also points of tangency with the utility theory.

Even as a user is inclined to choose the solution that requires the least effort from her she may, however, be unaware of all the possible solutions and the effort they carry and, therefore, will make her estimation on what she believes carries the least effort. Furthermore, selecting the solution that carries the least effort is not necessarily preceded by much reflection on all possible solutions. Hence, the solution that a user chooses may not be the solution with the actual lowest effort, but what she ***perceives*** to be the option of ***least effort***. When estimating which solution carries the least effort, the user should consider not only the implications of the choice at the present moment, but also the future implications of her choice. Selecting a solution that would require very little amount of work or effort today may result in a situation that requires increased amounts of work in the future. Similarly, a user may choose to make a higher effort today in order to have less work tomorrow. Therefore, in order to invest as little effort as possible, people need to consider future implications of their current actions. Future choices of the individual are affected by whether the effort level of previous choices corresponded to her estimations [8]. Ultimately, a rational user will choose the solution that in the long run carries the lowest perceived effort (including time, money and energy spent).

In actuality the decision to select a solution may be made based on the effort needed to make the selection and the effort required by the selected solution; this implies that if all solutions' characteristics are not known to the user, then finding out those characteristics to determine which solution actually is the best may be perceived to require more effort than selecting the least effort solution of the "well known solutions".

3.3 The Lazy User Model in Relation to Other Technology Acceptance and Adoption Theories

The Lazy User Model presented in the previous section has been defined according to the following propositions: (i) the user need is very specific, can be fulfilled 100%, and defines the number of available solutions, (ii) the user state limits the number of solutions, (iii) the user has to choose between several competing solutions, and (iv) the least perceived effort is the underlying rationale for the user selection process. In section 2, we reviewed several theories on user acceptance and adoption of technology. We summarize the characteristics of these models in Table 1.

Table 1. A comparison of technology acceptance and adoption theories

Components	TRA	TAM	UTAUT	TTF	DOI	Cognitive Fit	Lazy User
Voluntariness of use (the degree to which use of the innovation is perceived as being voluntary)			X		X		X
Specific user need							X
Characteristics of the user (age, gender, cultural and social belonging)							X
Gender			X				X
Experience			X			X	X
Age			X				X
Social influence/Image (degree to which the individual perceives he or she could use a system and how others will view her as a result of using)	X		X		X		X
Behavioural intention/Attitude toward act or behaviour/Mental representation of the problem	X	X	X			X	
Problem solving skill (not experience)						X	
Circumstances surrounding the user (location, available time, available resources)							X
Facilitating conditions/Compatibility (perceived organizational or infrastructural support to use system, innovation consistent with existing values), pre+during use			X		X		X
Perceived effort (time+cost+energy of choosing a specific solution), pre-use							X
Perceived ease of use/effort expectancy (of technology), pre-use		X	X		X		X
Perceived usefulness/performance expectancy/Relative advantage, (the degree to which an individual believes that using the system will help her to attain gains in job performance), pre-use		X	X		X		X
Performance impacts (the perceived impact of a system on performance), post-use				X			X
Utilization (the proportion of times users choose to use a specific system, showing good/poor fit)				X			
Trialability/divisibility (the degree to which an innovation may be tried on a limited basis)					X		
Result demonstrability (the more perceived advantages, the more likely to be adopted)					X		
Visibility (actual visibility of the innovation)					X		
Task characteristics				X		X	
Technology characteristics/External representation of problem (e.g. graph)				X		X	
Focus on problem solving						X	X
Focus on fit (between task + process/technology)				X		X	
Focus on usage behaviour, intention to use	X	X	X				
User focus (possibly many solutions)			X			X	X
Technology focus (one solution/technology)	X	X	X	X	X		

Compared to other theories, LUM does not explicitly take into account (i) behavioral intention (a theme largely represented in other theories), (ii) actual utilization level, triability, and result demonstrability (which relate to how using a solution for a limited amount of time may lead to further adoption), and (iii) task and technology characteristics. One of the distinguishing factors of LUM is that it focuses on several competing solutions, and hence, is a dynamic model of solution selection, whereas other theories focus on one solution or technology.

4 Discussion about Switching and Learning Costs in the Lazy User Model Framework

The perceived effort in Lazy User Model is affected by the user state in every individual situation. The user state includes also the user specific switching and learning costs, as perceived by the user. Switching costs have been studied and developed extensively in economics and marketing. Economic research has focused on the "potential competitive implications" of switching costs, whereas marketing research has focused on "the implications of switching costs from a customer behaviour standpoint and customer retention" [30]. Information systems has mainly followed the economic research approach [30].

4.1 Switching Costs

When facing a decision to change from one solution to another, users must weigh the costs of switching: these are called switching costs. In economic and management literature, switching costs have been defined as "the costs associated with switching suppliers" [31]. These costs include time, effort and knowledge that the customer invests in a product, service or relationship [32].

Switching costs include (adapted from Hess and Ricart, [32]): *durable purchase* (e.g., a software one-time license or acquisition), *complementary purchase* (e.g., software add-ons, peripherals), *relationship* (e.g., investment made in developing a relationship with the solution supplier, which could result in accumulated knowledge, expertise, contracted short or long-term service agreement and/or attachment), *learning/training* (e.g., initial learning, problem-solving knowledge acquired over time), *search costs* (e.g., investment made to find the solution supplier and to learn about the characteristics of the supplier and its offering), *psychological* (e.g., attachment, resistance to change), *network and critical mass* (e.g., the fact that there is a large enough customer base using the solution), *trust, risk of failure* (if the new solution does not perform as expected), *switching back costs, information management* (e.g., if the new solution requires to move data to a new database).

It is to be noted that these costs are not necessarily either high or low, but these can be identified and perhaps placed on a continuum, where different degrees of costs exist. Also costs are not static, but change dynamically over time (e.g., learning costs, where knowledge is accumulated over time; or acquisition costs, which can change if the user can benefit from a temporary promotional offer).

In their study, Hess and Ricart [32] identify three types of costs: costs created by previous investments, costs created by potential investments, and opportunity costs. Some investments are so-called sunk investments (i.e., these cannot be redeemed when the user decides to use another solution). Some investments are transferable (e.g., a user can transfer part of its knowledge when using a new service with a similar interface as the previous solution, therefore requiring less learning). This has several implications for our framework:

Users will make a trade-off between previous investments and future possible investments: if a new solution is to be adopted by a user, the future investment and its associated returns will have to outweigh the benefits of previous investments. In other words, the marginal gain must be high enough in order to promote a leap in productivity).

Users will favor using solutions, where part of their previous investments can be transferred in order to ease the adoption process of that new solution.

Because the framework is dynamic (the user might switch back to a previous solution depending on its state and need), the user will try to avoid lock-in situations and favor the use of solution where switching costs are minimal; this could even be called "keeping options open". Understanding why users switch is also an important issue, when investigating the solution selection process. In terms of switching costs; it is interesting to know which costs are the barriers to a possible switch, and what triggers switching.

Research has shown that experience with one solution (and therefore associated learning) raises the cost of switching to another. In Johnson et al. [33], switching costs are modeled with the concept of "cognitive lock-in". When learning to use one solution, high cognitive costs are incurred by the user: these are sunk investments. After several uses, as the user finds out more efficient ways to use the solution and performance increases, cognitive costs slowly decrease; however, at this stage, a situation of cognitive lock-in has occurred since it does not make sense to switch to another solution – note that repeated use of the solution leads to economies of scale for the user because the marginal cost of continuing to use the solution is lower than switching. Johnson et al. [33] also demonstrate that proficient users of a website are more likely to purchase through this particular website than through another. It should also be added that, as Murray and Häubl [34] demonstrate, cognitive switching costs do not apply to the whole extent of functionality of the solution: for example, a user might learn to use only a specific subset of the whole functionality, hence engaging in cognitive lock-in for this subset. If a competing solution fulfills needs not met by this specific subset, cognitive lock-in and sunk costs are negligible and do not constitute a barrier to a change of solution.

4.2 Learning Issues

As part of the switching costs, we mentioned learning and training as important factors. In the following, we attempt to describe how these costs materialize in the solution selection and adoption process. We identify four learning phases in the solution adoption process:

- Pre-usage, before a solution is selected.
- First time of use
- Early use
- Routine use. Adoption cycle and learning (from first use to routine use ⇨ sunk cost)

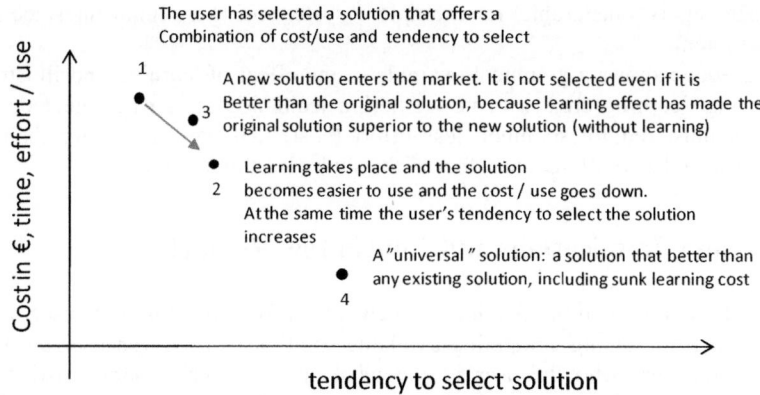

Fig. 2. Learning decreases the effort of use and increases the tendency to select a solution

In the pre-usage phase, users need information about the solution: that information might be related to the use of solution itself, or it might also be related to other aspects of the solution, such as financial costs. If we consider learning investments at this stage, users might be interested in several issues (e.g. how easy the system is to use, how easy it is to learn to use, what the experiences of peer users are, what the possible drawbacks are). It is during this stage that expectations about system performance and usability are created. The channels through which users learn about a solution are many, but the most important might be through existing documentation or word of mouth.

The first time of use is often pivotal in the adoption process. It is often said that the first impression matters a lot in how we make our judgments. It is during the first use that the users will be able to compare their expectations about system use with the actual use. This comparison is often done "on the spot" and might be based on positive or negative experiences of the system, because users usually remember only "highs" or "lows" during system use. The end result might be that the user accepts or rejects the system. This phase is crucial since it can be difficult to change the user's willingness to use if he has built a negative attitude towards a system.

During the early use phase, the user will establish a knowledge base which will lead him towards the routine use of the system. Based on the early experiences the user learns in more detail how the solution works, discovers new features and develops problem-solving skills and strategies (in case she runs into problems).

In the last phase (routine use), the user knows how to use the functions she needs and can use routinely the system without committing any major errors. The user does not know how to use all the functions of the system (few users actually do), but she knows how to solve problems. The user focuses on keeping up-to-date his knowledge about the system.

This learning process illustrates the different phases where the user has to make a learning investment. Each of these learning investments (acquiring knowledge, gaining experience, learning to use, developing problem solving skills and strategies, updating knowledge about the system) is different in nature: they require different levels of effort and happen at different points of time in the learning process. Part of these investments is transferable; for example, a system using a similar interface than a previous system.

Figure 2 above shows a graphical example of the effect of learning and illustrates the barrier that learning creates to new entering technologies. To be selected, new technologies must require so much less effort (cost) that they are better than the solution in use and also off-set the effect of the sunk effort in learning.

5 Discussion, Implications and Concluding Remarks

Lazy User Model for solution selection is a new model for explaining how users make their selection from among competing available solutions for a given user problem. The model considers who the user is and what are the user's characteristics and resources and in what kind of a situation the user finds herself in. Information about the user can be used in limiting the set of available solutions to feasible alternatives. The model postulates that the user selects a solution for her problem from the feasible set of solutions by selecting the solution that inflicts the least effort. Effort is the individually, by the user, constituted combination measure for the monetary cost, physical or cognitive effort, and time consumption that each of the solutions (are perceived to) requires by the user.

The literature on user acceptance and adoption of technologies is wide, with a number of different models that approach the issue. There is however room for new approaches, like the Lazy User Model, that integrate the user perspective and selection of solutions from a set of competing solutions, and use a "selection criteria" from outside the realm of technology - technology does not choose, technology is chosen by the user.

Switching costs and learning play a role in technology acceptance and adoption, the more a user uses a given solution the better she is likely to be able to use it the next time round; it has also been shown that there is a correlation between proficiency of use and financial returns from the solution provider perspective (e.g. more fluent users of a specific website are more likely to purchase on this website). This learning effect lowers the effort level required by using of a given solution and makes the solution more likely to be accepted, even when new solutions become available. The Lazy User Model is able to treat the learning effect in considering the changed selection situation and brings insight by being able to show to how learning, as a sunk investment, creates switching costs and how "user lock-in" situations can develop. Literature also illustrates that switching costs related to learning are very complex, and can be applicable to only a subset of a solution's functionality.

We feel that the Lazy User Model brings many new insights to the technology adoption and acceptance literature and opens avenues for further research about understanding the importance of learning and the switching costs to the design of technology; such research is warmly welcomed by Benbasat and Barki [19]. As such the Lazy User Model is a good addition to the toolbox of researchers and analysts for defining the playing field and niches for prospective new solutions (technologies and products).

The implications of this research are twofold: (i) first, an understanding of the solution selection process and its related factors allow us to create a tool that can be used by practitioners (for example, mobile service providers) to evaluate how their prospective new solution is going to fit in a market where there are other competing solutions available, and therefore to identify the thresholds that new solutions must overcome in order to be adopted (for example, by identifying and implementing strategies to attract or lock-in users by managing the switching costs), (ii) solution designers can use the model in order to understand the limiting conditions and the user needs in order to design new services that require the »least effort« from the user's point of view, and that will be successful on the market.

Further work will include further validation of the model with an in-depth study. This validation work will be the basis for refining the model and creating an evaluation tool for mobile service providers.

References

1. Davis, F.D.: Perceived Usefulness, Perceived Ease of Use, and User Acceptance of Information Technology. MIS Quarterly 13, 319–340 (1989)
2. Bagozzi, R.P., et al.: Development and Test of a theory of technological learning and usage. Human Relations 45, 660–686 (1992)
3. Venkatesh, V., et al.: User acceptance of information technology: Toward a unified view. MIS Quarterly 27, 425–478 (2003)
4. Goodhue, D.L.: Understanding User Evaluations of Information Systems. Management Science 41, 1827–1844 (1995)
5. Goodhue, D.L., Thompson, R.L.: Task-technology fit and individual performance. MIS Quarterly 19, 213–236 (1995)
6. Vessey: Cognitive Fit: A Theory-Based Analysis of the Graphs Versus Tables Literature. Decision Sciences 22, 219–240 (1991)
7. Vessey, Galletta, D.F.: Cognitive Fit: An Empirical Study of Information Acquisition. Information Systems Research 2, 63–84 (1991)
8. Zipf, G.K.: Human Behavior and the Principle of Least Effort. Addison-Wesley, Reading (1949)
9. Ferrer i Cancho, R., Solé, R.V.: Least effort and the origins of scaling in human language. Proceedings of the National Academy of Sciences of the United States of America 100, 788–791 (2003)
10. Mann, T.: A Guide to Library Research Methods. Oxford University Press, USA (1987)
11. Team, T.L.: Lazy Users and Automatic Video Retrieval Tools in (the) Lowlands. In: 10th Text Retrieval Conference, TREC, Gaithersburg, Maryland, USA (2001)
12. Chu, D., et al.: UVa Bus.NET: Enhancing User Experiences on Smart Devices through Context-Aware Computing. In: 2004 IEEE Consumer Communications and Networking Conference, Las Vegas, Nevada, USA, pp. 511–515 (2004)
13. Raghavan, R., et al.: InterActive Feature Selection. In: 19th International Joint Conference on Artificial Intelligence, Edinburgh, Scotland, UK (2005)
14. Franks, J., Sussman, O.: Financial Distress and Bank Restructuring of Small to Medium Size UK Companies. Review of Finance 9, 65–96 (2005)
15. Fishbein, M., Azjen, I.: Belief, Attitude and Behavior: an Introduction to Theory and Reseach. Addison-Wesley, Reading (1975)

16. Sheppard, B., et al.: The Theory of Reasoned Action: A Meta-Analysis of Past Research with Recommendations for Modifications and Future Research. The Journal of Consumer Research 15, 325–343 (1988)
17. Rogers, E.M.: Diffusion of Innovations, 5th edn. Free Press, New York (2003)
18. Moore, G.C., Benbasat, I.: Development of an Instrument to Measure the Perceptions of Adopting an Information Technology Innovation. Information Systems Research 2, 192–222 (1991)
19. Benbazat, Barki, H.: Quo vadis, TAM. Journal of the Association for Information Systems 8(4), 211–218 (2007)
20. Collan, M.: Lazy User Behaviour. In: RePEc 2007 (2007)
21. Collan, M., Tetard, F.: Lazy User Theory of Solution Selection. In: CELDA 2007, Algarve, Portugal, pp. 273–279 (2007)
22. Tétard, F.: Lazy User Theory: A Dynamic Model to Understand User Selection of Products and Services. In: 42nd Hawaii International Conference on System Sciences, HICSS-42, Hawaii (2009)
23. Collan, M., et al.: Understanding the User Selection Process of Mobile Services with the Lazy User Model: An Exploratory Study. In: GMR 2009 - Global Mobility Roundtable 2009, Cairo, Egypt (2009)
24. Zanette, D.: Zipf's law and the creation of musical context. Musicae Scientiae 10, 3–18 (2006)
25. Reichle, E., et al.: The Neural Bases of Strategy and Skill in Sentence - Picture Verification. Cognitive Psychology 40, 261–295 (2000)
26. Constantinou: Consumer behaviour and Advanced Mobile data Services: Opening the "Black Box" of the Individual's Choice Process. International Journal of Social and Humanistic Computing 1, 67–80 (2008)
27. Kotler, P.: Marketing Management: Analysis, Planning, Implementation, and Control, 9th edn. Prentice-Hall, Upper Saddle River (1997)
28. Newell, Simon, H.A.: Human Problem Solving. Prentice-Hall, Englewood Cliffs (1972)
29. Collan, M., et al.: Using E- and M-Busines Components in Business: Approaches, Cases, and Rules of Thumb. In: Lee, I. (ed.) Electronic Business: Concepts, Methodologies, Tools, and Applications, vol. 1, pp. 550–564. IGI Publishing, Hershey (2009)
30. Chen, P.-Y., Hitt, L.M.: Information Technology and Switching Costs. In: Hendershott, T. (ed.) Handbooks in Information Systems. Economics and Information Systems, vol. 1, pp. 437–470. Elsevier, Amsterdam (2006)
31. Thompson, R.L., Cats-Baril, W.: Information Technology and Management. McGraw-Hill, New York (2002)
32. Hess, M., Ricart, J.E.: Managing Customer Switching Costs: a Framework for Competing in the Networked Environment. Management Research 1, 93–110 (Winter 2002-2003)
33. Johnson, E., Bellman, S., Lohse, G.: Cognitive Lock-in and the Power Law of Practice. Journal of Marketing 67, 62–75 (2003)
34. Murray, K., Häubl, G.: Explaining Cognitive Lock-In: the Role of Skill-Based Habits of Use in Consumer Choice. Journal of Consumer Research 34(1), 77–88 (2007)

Tactics for Producing Actionable Information

Torstein E.L. Hjelle and Eric Monteiro

Department of Computer and Information Science, Norwegian University of Science and
Technology (NTNU), Trondheim, Norway
{torstein.hjelle,eric.monteiro}@idi.ntnu.no

Abstract. Exploitation and production of oil and gas involve significant human,
environmental and economical risks. Everyday concerns – Should we drill
further down? Maybe inject more water? Why is the well producing these
amounts of sand? – rely on vast amounts of structured and unstructured
information accessible in different formats, applications and platforms. This
information is never perfect: there are missing/ unavailable information,
inaccuracies and errors, in short, there are uncertainties tied to the information.
Our primary question is, how do engineers – in practice – cope under these
conditions? We contribute by (i) identifying tactics for making information
credible and trustworthy enough for daily operations i.e. strategies to transform
"mere" information into actionable information as well as (ii) drawing out
practical implications of our analysis.

Keywords: Integration, trust, interdisciplinary collaboration.

1 Introduction

If nothing else, the recent accident with the BP operated oil drilling rig Deepwater
Horizon in the Gulf of Mexico vividly illustrated the threats to human life, the
environment and the economy posed by deep sea oil and gas production. Oil and gas
companies are extremely information intensive operations. They rely on truly vast
amounts of information, e.g. seismic data, geological models, reservoir models,
simulations, drilling logs, production measurements, intervention reports and process
parameters, for their everyday operations. In principle, daily operations of an oil and
gas field are based on "all" this information. In practice, there are a number of
impediments. The *amount* of information is staggering not to say prohibitive for
careful analysis. Moreover, the extensive number of databases, applications and
platforms containing this information is in part fragmented, redundant and
inconsistent rather than as seamlessly integrated as advocates of technological fixes to
integration tout. In addition, the information contains errors and/ or inaccuracies that
entail it cannot be trusted at face value. What, then, do practitioners do to cope?

The aim of this paper is to (i) identify tactics employed by users when producing
actionable information from information that is overwhelming, poorly integrated and
often inaccurate and (ii) to draw out practical implications of our analysis.

Empirically we study the everyday work of two of the principal professional
communities involved in oil and gas operations, viz. production and reservoir

H. Salmela and A. Sell (Eds.): SCIS 2011, LNBIP 86, pp. 69–83, 2011.

engineers. They plan and fine-tune the running of oil and gas wells on a daily basis. Our case company is a 30.000 employee Fortune 500 company OGC (Oil and Gas Company, a pseudonym for anonymity) operating in 40 countries, a large international energy company with focus on gas and oil production. OGC is the world's largest operator on ocean depths of more than 100 meters.. Due to the limited potential for growth in its home region, OGC is actively seeking to grow globally.

The rest of the paper is organized as follows. Section 2 reviews relevant literature. Section 3 describes our research methods and background for the case. Our analysis in section 4, followed by the discussion in section 5, is organised around strategies for coping with (i) missing/ unavailable information, (ii) inaccurate or erroneous information and (iii) situations where previous knowledge do not apply. The last section offers concluding remarks.

2   Making Operational Sense of Information in Business Organisations

The running of any business is based on extensive information. Recent interest in e.g. business intelligence (see MISQ Special Issue on Business Intelligence Research [1]) is motivated by the prospects of having available relevant information at your fingertips, as it were. This would enable different types of analyses helpful to the running of the business with subsequent sound actions based on this. The problem, however, is that such an approach abstracts away from real-world issues with fragmented, potentially inconsistent and inaccurate data. Business intelligence *assumes* that information quality is adequate, and proceeds to look at ways to massage, manipulate and present views of the information. We are concerned with situations where strong assumptions about information quality do not hold.

A key reason why at least larger business organizations struggle with data quality is the *heterogeneity* of the information: a large number of applications, modules, formats and databases that have been set up over many years. Such collections of information systems tend to be fragmented by historical and organizational reasons and they stubbornly resist many attempts of integration. Or, "Rather, the information is spread across dozens or even hundreds of separate computer systems, each housed in an individual function, business unit, region, factory or office" as formulated by [2].

Technical approaches to integration of large collections or portfolios of information systems dominate. "Integration has been the Holy Grail of MIS since the early days of computers in organizations" as pointed out by [3]. Over the last decades, a rich and expanding repertoire of technical mechanisms for integration has been proposed, from low-level (e.g., database schema integration), to middle-level (e.g., middle-ware like CORBA, Web services), to high-level (e.g., Service-Oriented Architectures (SOA)) solutions [4]. Yet organizational implementation lags significantly behind these promised returns [5-9]. Traditional approach to integration, in short, remains overly optimistic, prescriptive, and programmatic.

Some scholars have argued that tighter integration of information systems is unattainable as it but expresses an inherent socio-technical complexity [10]. A central tenet here is how integration triggers unintended consequences that fuel escalating complexity [11]. In short, this complexity makes information imperfect, or as Law dramatically phrases it "There are always many imperfections. And to make perfection in one place (assuming such a thing was possible) would be to risk much greater imperfection in other locations...The argument is that entropy is chronic" [12].

Within such a theoretical perspective, the prospects of integrated information systems appear gloomy. In empirical cases, however, users display ingenuity and improvisations rather than despair. How do practitioners cope with these (inherent?) imperfections in the information in their everyday work? The literature points out a number of resources to draw on.

First, information underpinning decisions and action need to be trusted. Not only the content of the information matters, also who produced it i.e. the identity of the source. This reiterates [13]'s point about the deeply social character of knowledge in the sense that: "Insofar as knowledge comes to us via other people's relations, taking in that knowledge, rejecting it, or holding judgment in abeyance involves knowledge of who these people are. ... What of relevance to credibility assessment do we know about them as individuals and as members of some collectivity?".

Second, robust knowledge is produced through collective and manual deliberations with peers. This involves, as [14] point out, an element of validating or sense-making of the different elements: "In summary then, the problem of integration of knowledge in knowledge-intensive firms is not a problem of simply combining, sharing or making data commonly available. It is a problem of perspective taking in which the unique thought worlds of different communities of knowing are made visible and accessible to others".

Third, the kind of trust involved in knowledge work is not a static entity either present or absent. It is rather the performed achievement of a concerted and highly heterogeneous effort with actors, artefacts and other externalised knowledge representations. As pointed out by [15], "the perceived value of medical information is related to the perceived credibility of the source". An important aspect of knowledge work, then, is to unpack how disembedded or externalised knowledge representations are rendered credible and trustworthy.

In sum, approaches to the use of operationally relevant information in business like business intelligence tend to gloss over how information, in and of itself, is not immediately trustworthy i.e. actionable. Users of information draw on social networks to filter the information. Still, a more detailed identification of tactics employed is lacking for users such as the engineers we study inside OGC.

3 Case

3.1 Setting

As most industries, the oil and gas industry is interested in maximizing profit. And as OGC has little influence on the price they get per barrel, the only way to maximize profit is to either produce more or reduce costs. As there is a finite number of oil fields available, production can only be increased by draining a larger portion of oil and gas from the existing reservoirs. Another option is to produce oil and gas more efficiently, i.e. produce more oil and gas per euro spent. A report from the national oil industry association indicated a pent-up potential of more than 30 billion Euros. Hence, an initiative to release this potential was kicked off early this century. The ambition was to increase recovery by supporting people in making better decisions quicker through improvements in both collaboration and communication.

One outcome of this initiative has been an increased use of collaboration technology. Most meeting rooms have been equipped with big screens, projectors and interactive whiteboards (i.e. Smart Boards). Being able to use technology to get together, share and work on the same information was believed to improve collaboration and lead to better decisions. In addition, many meeting rooms were equipped with video conferencing facilities.

In Northern Europe OGC have 3 operations centres. Each centre operates a number of oil and gas fields in the North Sea. This research has followed a group of people responsible for two such oil and gas fields. This group is responsible for ensuring optimal drainage of the two fields combined with optimal utilization of the available processing facilities. They both plan and follow up production on both a day-to-day basis, as well as on longer terms. They are responsible for planning and implementing well operations in order to ensure stable and reliable production, as well as preparing weekly and yearly production plans. In short, they are responsible for getting as much oil and gas from the reservoir under the seabed to the processing facilities either on a platform or onshore – given the limitations of each individual well, a group of wells, processing facilities or corporate policies.

All in all there are about 25 people working in this group. A number of disciplines are included in this group: Production engineers, reservoir engineers, petro physicists, geophysicists and geologists. The focuses of the different disciplines vary. For instance, the production focuses more on the everyday production of oil and gas as compared to most of the others who focus more on finding more oil and gas in new and existing reservoirs. The reservoir engineers are somewhere in between these extremes and contribute both in long term planning and short term production.

All members of the group are co-located. They work in a large open plan office where the desks are grouped together in threes – with the exception of 4 production engineers who work in a separate collaboration room separated from the rest of the group by a large sliding door. In addition to the 4 work stations, each with three monitors, this room is equipped with 2 projectors, an interactive whiteboard and one 42-46" LCD monitor. The content on any of the monitors at the workstations can be displayed and shared on any of the large screen in the room. The room is also equipped with video conference facilities. This room is used for internal group meetings, as well as with people from outside the group if the meeting is related to production. Except for during meetings, the sliding door is most often left open.

The reason these production engineers sit in a separate room is mainly because they are responsible for the daily operations and interact more often with people from outside the group. For instance, it is the production engineers who most often interact with the people offshore on the platform or with people controlling the process plants.

As mentioned, the group is responsible for two oil and gas fields. Both are quite new. The oldest began production in 2005 and are currently producing from 12 individual wells. The field is mainly a gas producing field and produces very little oil. This field produces from a reservoir with higher pressure and temperature than any other field in the North Sea. The second field began production in the summer of

2009. It currently has 4 production wells in addition to one gas injection well. New wells are still being planned, drilled and put into production. This field produces mainly oil and is expected to be in production until 2029. Both fields are mainly subsurface installations connected to a common platform where the production is processed before being shipped away.

Fulfilling production goals on a week-by-week basis is in many ways what the group gets measured by. It is by far the most visible and easily understandable metric to measure success or failure. Working together to ensure good results is thus important. As mentioned, the production engineers handle the production aspect of the operations. One of their more important is every week to produce a production plan for the coming week. Simply put, this plan tells how much oil and gas they expect to produce the upcoming week. Knowing this is important to other parts of OGC; for instance the units who are responsible for processing, transporting or selling the oil and gas. If they don't know exactly how much oil and gas that is to be produced they will not know how to manage it.

In order to do their job efficiently the production engineers rely on good collaboration with especially the reservoir engineers. The production engineers create and maintain reservoir models - both for each individual well and the entire reservoir. These models are continuously updated and modified. The main purpose of the models is to predict the behaviour of the wells and reservoir in order to know how much oil and gas a well can produce and at what rate.

To decide how to best run a well, the production engineers and reservoir engineers have a dedicated management forum that meets about once every two weeks for approximately two hours to discuss the current status of the field, each individual well and how to run it in the upcoming period. As input to these meetings the production engineers bring with them the current status of field and wells, the production details for the last period and the results of any tests done the last period. The reservoir engineers bring with them modified and up to date reservoir models.

3.2 Methods

This paper reports from findings in an ongoing interpretive case study [16] where we look at how people conduct their everyday work in order to assign meaning and understand the rationale behind their actions.

3.2.1 Data Collection
Data collection has consisted of (i) observations, (ii) semi-structured interviews and (iii) document analysis and has been conducted from early 2007 to August 2010.

Observations

Observations began in earnest in March 2009 when we got access to a group of engineers working with oil and gas production. During our observation period we visited OGC about 110 days. During the observations we followed their daily work routine. We were allowed to sit in during meetings, both internal meeting within the group and with external partners. In total, more than 375 meetings, ranging from 3 minute long status updates to day-long work sessions, were observed. Table 1 summarizes the meetings observed.

Table 1. Summary of types of meetings observed

Meeting type	Frequency	Duration	Participants	Purpose
Control room meeting	Daily	15-25 minutes	8-12	Production related events last and coming 24 hours
Platform meeting	Daily	15 minutes	18-22	Platform related events last and coming 24 hours
Petroleum technology	Daily	3-15 minutes	15-30	Summary of the two previous meetings with focus on petroleum technology
Production meeting	Weekly	1-2 hours	15-20	Planning activities and operations for the coming week
Reservoir meeting	Bi-weekly	2 hours	6-12	Status of fields and well, planning activities for the next period
Various meetings	Occasional	5 minutes – 6 hours	4 – 20	E.g. reservoir drainage strategy workshop

When not in meetings we were given access to work stations in the engineers' open plan office where we could work while still being able to be a part of the surroundings. This way we got the opportunity to observe how the engineers worked in their everyday work.

During observations handwritten notes were taken down. Either after the meetings or at the end of the day the notes were then written out. Thoughts and reflections made during the observations have been written down in a separate column in our notes. Questions were asked to clarify and elaborate findings, as deemed important by [17]. In order not to disturb meetings, these questions were most often asked while walking to or from meetings, or during lunch or breaks.

During these meetings, our role was purely observational. With one exception: The bi-weekly reservoir meetings. This meeting is a forum that was established during our period of observation and the group leaders wanted our input in order to make the forum as good as possible. So, at the end of each meeting, we spent a few minutes commenting on the meeting structure, organization, flow, etc.

Interviews

The second method of data collection has been semi-structured interviews. The initial interviews were quite open-ended and targeted at ICT professionals and lower to middle management. The aim was to get an understanding of various tools and systems available within the collaboration infrastructure and the rationale behind the decisions to implement and roll out the solutions they did.

The latter part of the interviews has been with the engineers at the operations centre. Here we have interviewed a variety of both junior and senior engineers within the disciplines of production, reservoir and process.

In total we have conducted 26 formal interviews, with 14 in the first part and 12 in the latter, lasting from 1 to 3 hours. Only 8 of the interviews have been recorded, but as we in most interviews have been more than one researcher present, we have divided the task so that one is only focusing on writing down what is being said, and thus we have to some extent compensated for the lack of recordings. After the non-recorded interviews we immediately after the interview went through the notes together and clarified uncertainties.

Document Analysis

The third data collection method has been document analysis. We carried out an extensive study of presentations, formal descriptions of work processes, plans and strategies, both related to the collaboration infrastructure and to oil and gas production. This analysis gave us a good understanding of the information infrastructure; and the possibilities and limitations set by this.

3.2.2 Data Analysis
Our data analysis is a never-ending, continuous process. By overlapping data analysis and data collection we have been able to achieve added flexibility [18]. Our field notes have been very important. As suggested by [19] we have separated our 'raw' data from our own comments, reflections and questions. Seeing that we, as researchers, are influenced by our previous experiences and backgrounds, this has influenced our analysis. Through inductive work, our analytical categories have materialized from both internal discussions and with discussions with researchers at OGC, as well as reading of field notes.

The first-order conceptualizing [19] began at the field site. Often, as we had reflected on our observations, we used this as a basis for further discussions and issues to pursue. Our data was manually coded and in turn categorized, similar to the process of constant comparison found in grounded theory. By using a bottom-up categorization strategy focusing on functions of quality practices, we developed an interpretive template as shown in table 2 that we use in the subsequent section.

Discussing early findings with both the engineers and other researchers provided valuable validation as the engineers could confront our interpretations. These sessions have helped ensure that we have understood the engineers' world as thoroughly as possible.

Table 2. Our interpretative template derived through a combination of bottom-up, open coding and classification of data with deductive elements

Construct	Evidence, example
Filling the gaps	*"We probably don't have a clue what the gas-oil ratio is, and at what rate."*
Coping with inaccuracies	*"Just ignore this point. It is an inaccurate test."*
Dealing with the unexpected	*"Well W3 doesn't produce water"* when faced with measurements suggesting so.

4 Analysis

Even though the production engineers and reservoir engineers have access to a lot of different tools and systems that provide them with data they still have challenges they need to sort out in order to make their job as good as possible. To meet these challenges the group have developed a series of strategies and workarounds.

4.1 Filling the Gaps

During our time with the engineers we observed them having a number of problems with various types of measurement equipment. One such occasion was shortly after production began on the newest oil and gas field. Just a few weeks after being started, the contact with the subsea measurement equipment on two wells got lost. As these two wells were connected to the same production line (together with two other wells) they had no way of actually getting to know the individual properties of the two well without closing down at least one well – and thus lose production. For instance, they were not able to measure how much oil and gas the two wells produced respectively, nor could they measure the pressure or temperature from the two wells individually. As the wells had only been in production for a couple of weeks they had very little historically data. This meant that they had very little knowledge of the situation that they could use to compensate for the broken equipment.

As it is important to know how much oil and gas each well is producing in order for the reservoir engineers to create and maintain accurate reservoir models the lack of information was often discussed during meetings.

In one reservoir management meeting a couple of weeks after the loss of the equipment the leading reservoir engineer addressed the problem of the faulty equipment and how to compensate. The leading reservoir engineer wanted to know how long it would take to get the equipment repaired or replaced. The production coordinator informed that according to the last information he had, it would take several months.

The discussion then revolved around how they would cope until the situation was mended. As the leading reservoir engineer pointed out, to the reservoir engineers the time shortly after startup is important in order to see if things are evolving as expected. If not they would have to update their models and projections. *"We probably don't have a clue what the gas-oil ratio is, and at what rate."* He then suggested closing down one of the wells with the faulty equipment for a short time in order to get the missing data. If they closed down one of the two wells they would be able to at least measure the how much oil and gas the wells produced by taking the total for the three wells and subtracting the production from the two wells with functioning equipment, giving the production rate for the third well. And by taking the total production from all four wells and subtracting the total for the three wells they would know the production from the fourth well.

However, the leading production engineer argued that the benefits would not outweigh the production loss: They would not get any information about the pressures and temperatures in the wells, and that was the most important information. Then he ended with saying *"We are too hung up on details on [field two]. We have a lot of data. If [field two] had been a field without down-hole gauges and multi phase meters nobody would have worried about this."*

Production coordinator, whose screen was being displayed on a projection screen, used instant messaging to query the operations engineer about whether some maintenance planned for the next week would cause any production restrictions. The operations engineer answered that it was likely. The production coordinator then suggested that they use this opportunity to close down one of the wells and get the measurements. The leading reservoir engineer accepted this as a compromise, but insisted that they should push on to have the equipment repaired or replaced quickly.

4.2 Coping with Inaccuracies

For a period of several months the group had problems with detectors registering that one of the wells were producing sand. Sand in this setting is pieces of solid matter, i.e. tiny fragments of rock from the reservoir. Getting sand into the production is problematic because of the sand's eroding properties. The sand passing through the pipes at high speeds would over time grind down the insides of the pipes, eventually breaking through the pipe and cause a leak. Depending on the location of the leak, this, in turn, could possibly lead to a dangerous situation onboard the platform, or a major spill with severe environmental consequences.

During one of the reservoir management meetings the group tried to figure out what was going on. This meeting was held in a room (See figure 1) with 6 workstations, all facing three projection screens on a wall. Each workstation had 2 monitors. All monitors could be displayed on each of projection screens. The leader, the production coordinator, two reservoir engineers and two production engineers occupied the workstations. Two more reservoir engineers and one production engineer sat on chairs between the people at the workstations.

The production coordinator began by summarizing what had been done to solve to problem: The well had been run on a separate line of the processing plant and no sand had been found. The detector had been reconfigured – to no avail. Then the detector had been replaced, but still they got indications of sand being produced.

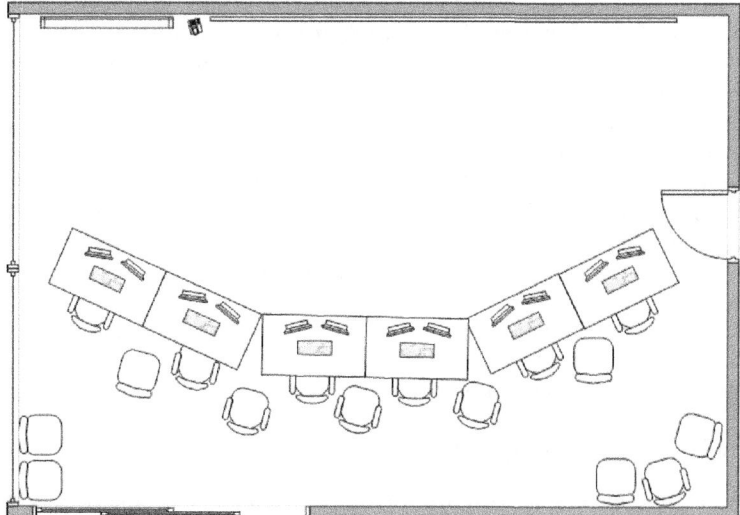

Fig. 1. Layout of meeting room

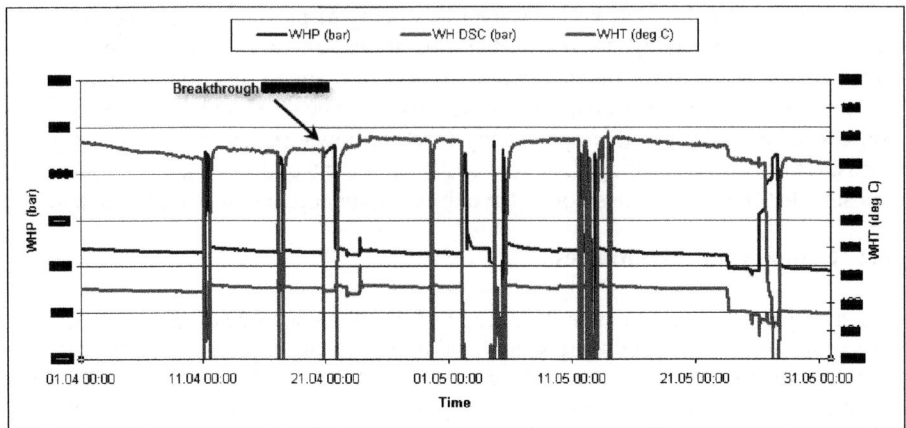

Fig. 2. Excerpt of slide presented by production engineer

Next, the production engineer responsible for that well pulled up a PowerPoint presentation on one of the projection screens. This presentation contained the analyses of the results of all tests conducted on that well since it began production. The presentation contained about 80 slides, but the production engineer quickly shipped to the last slide. Here he had inserted a screen dump from one of the production engineer's tools. The slide showed a graph with a number of lines (See excerpt in figure 2). Annotated arrows pointed to specific positions on the graphs. The production engineer referred to various points on the graphs and told that nothing else, i.e. temperature, pressure, oil-to-gas ratio or water content, had changed since the apparent occurrence of sand. One point on graph did however not match the rest, but he dismissed it saying *"Just ignore this point. It's an inaccurate test."* If the well had in fact been producing sand, he would have expected some changes.

The leader running the meeting then intervened and said *"Maybe we are trying too hard to prove that it is not producing sand. Maybe we should try to prove that it is producing sand?"* before asking if anybody else had something that could shed light upon the situation.

Then the reservoir engineer responsible for the reservoir area in question put his monitor on the projection screen. He then showed a model of the reservoir and told that according to their models there were no reasons for the well to produce sand. Other wells at similar depths in the same area did not produce any sand.

The production coordinator then summarized the situation; stating that since they did not find any physical sand from the well in the process plant and since they had no other indications of sand production they should conclude that there was no actual sand production from the well and that they had a false positive caused by some sort of interference. However, they would have to pay attention to the situation if something changed. Nobody disagreed.

4.3 Dealing with the Unexpected

Most of the time the engineers utilize their previous understanding of and knowledge about their oil and gas field in order to conduct their everyday work. However, sometimes their understanding and knowledge is either not comprehensive enough or simply not correct. When tweaking and adjusting information and models does not yield a sufficient understanding they have to use more drastic measures.

The reservoir engineers create, modify and maintain various models of both the entire reservoir and the individual wells. They also have models of various parts of the reservoir.

During a particularly intense reservoir management meeting where the engineers had difficulties agreeing how to run the field in the upcoming period, one of the more senior production engineers commented upon a graph in one of the reservoir engineers' model that showed water production from well W3 (a pseudonym). "Well W3 doesn't produce water", he said. The reservoir engineer responsible for this area of the reservoir then told that there was something wrong with the reservoir models for that area. Their initial prognoses showed that the reservoir would be so depleted within 4 to 6 months after start up that W3 would begin producing water. This had not happened. Whenever the models for the well were adjusted, the graph for water production was simply shifted forward in time (See figure 3).

A senior reservoir engineer then said that W3 was not the only well that did not produce water as anticipated. This was also the case with other wells in this part of the reservoir. But, as he said, *"The longer it takes before we begin producing water, the better"*. He then said that the normal history matching, or fine tuning, that they did on a regular basis did not manage to cater for this inaccuracy and that they needed to redo the reservoir models for the wells. However, they did not yet have had the time to do it as other tasks had had to be prioritized.

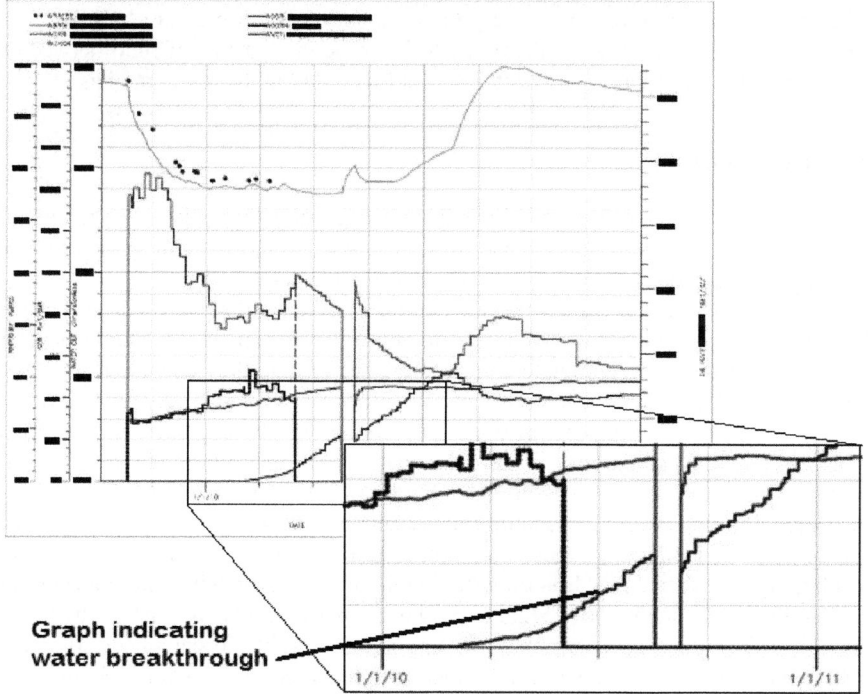

Fig. 3. Graph showing plot indicating water breakthrough

As just this meeting happened to be the first reservoir management meeting a newly-hired production engineer had attended, the leader running the meeting asked the senior reservoir engineer to say a bit about this task and possible reasons for doing it.

The reservoir engineers' task in such cases was to continuously adjust the various reservoir models by fine tuning them. Fine tuning a model involved matching the model with historical production data. Simply put, they would plot the various production data on a graph and then tweak, knead and stretch the models to fit those data as good as possible. However, sometimes it would be impossible to match actual production data with the model, like in the case of water production on W3. In order to correct for this, they would have to re-work the entire model. This was a much bigger task and required more time than they had available at the moment. If they needed to have it done quickly, it had to be initiated by management.

Further he told that there were many reasons why the models could be wrong. It could be that the initial models were simply wrong, i.e. they had an erroneous understanding of the reservoir's physical properties and had created a model with the wrong parameters. It could also be the case that the production from the reservoir had not been as anticipated. For instance, start up of other production wells may had been delayed, and thus, there would be more oil and gas left in the reservoir at the point in time when the model suggested the well should start producing water.

In this case, however, the senior reservoir engineer said that they suspected that there were some unexpected connections between two parts of the reservoir initially believed to be completely independent. When they had started injecting gas into this other part of the reservoir, they had gotten indications on a pressure build-up in the area with W3 as well. That is, there had to be some movements of fluid between the two areas. This was totally unexpected and not included in the initial models.

5 Discussion

As shown in the analysis above, oil and gas production is highly knowledge intensive work. The engineers rely on data and information from various sources and use their knowledge and understanding accumulated through experience.

The engineers need a variety of information in order to their job. Through various ICT tools and systems they get access to this information. In an ideal world they would have access to a complete and accurate set of data they could use in order to optimally produce oil and gas. However, the information the ICT systems provide are neither complete nor accurate. In order to compensate, the engineers utilize various strategies and tactics in order to ensure the quality and reliability of the information.

As is it near impossible to avoid that equipment breaks down, especially in difficult environments like oil and gas reservoirs where equipment have to deal with high fluctuations in both temperature and pressure, one cannot simply rely on reliable availability of information. It is important being able to cope when the information is not available. Thought the system does not provide redundancy as such, through domain knowledge and experience the engineers are able to calculate/estimate the missing information in a sufficient manner in order to get the job done. Being able to do so ensures that the engineers are able to run the wells in a safe and secure way, jeopardizing neither the well integrity, nor the safety of people or environment.

Due to the complexity of oil and gas production it is difficult to ensure that the equipment produce accurate information. For instance, identical sensors connected to the same pipe can yield different results simply based on the placement of the sensors, for instance if the sensors are placed before or after a bottleneck or on the inside or outside of a bend. This means that the engineers cannot routinely trust the information they get. Instead they have to validate the information before trusting it. As it is impossible to ensure 100 per cent validity or reliability, the engineers get to know through experience and domain knowledge when they have sufficiently validated the information.

Hands-on experience with an oil and gas reservoir with high temperatures and pressures deep below the seafloor is impossible. Thus models and simulations provide the engineers with their understanding of what is going on in the reservoir. As the understanding changes when they get more experience with the reservoir it is natural that the models need tweaking and at times major revisions.

6 Conclusions

Having all information, as it were, at your fingertips and trustworthy at face value seems a highly unlikely scenario as Porter convincingly argued [20]. This image abstracts away from the shortcuts, imperfections and glitches so typical for real-world knowledge-based, information intensive work. There are accordingly two ways to read the implications of our study.

On the one hand, the efforts to create perfectly accurate, available, consistent and complete information that decision- and action-taking automatically can trust seem futile [12]. Information is captured and stored in information systems for targeted purposes that make reuse of the same information later for different purposes challenging. For instance, during drilling you log details about drill pace and sediments whereas you in the later stage of production and reservoir planning are interested in the exact location where the well enters the reservoir.

On the other hand, the users are highly skilled and competent in working out what we in this paper describe as socio-technical strategies for assessing the uncertainties tied to the information. The futility of the efforts of "perfect" information pointed out above does not represent as bleak a prospect as it may appear. The users cope quite well with imperfect information even with complex and risky decisions; the strategies or heuristics employed compensate for the shortcomings of the information to create a socio-technically robust system for risk assessment that go well beyond nominal notions of "managing" risk. As part of their everyday practices, the production and reservoir engineers in our study balance the conflicting pressures stemming from increased short-term productivity, safety norms and professional judgment; they "shoulder the risk", to use Perin's phrase [21], by competently juggling the competing agendas.

In short, in order to conduct their work the engineers' knowledge must consist of *general knowledge* about oil and gas production, as well as *local knowledge* of the specific reservoirs and wells [22].

References

1. Chen, H., Chiang, R.H.L., Storey, V.C. (eds.): Business Intelligence Research. MISQ Special Issue (forthcoming)
2. Davenport, T.H.: Putting the enterprise into the enterprise system. Harvard Business Review 76(4), 121 (1998)
3. Kumar, K., Hillegersberg, J.v.: Enterprise resource planning: introduction. Commun. ACM 43(4), 22–26 (2000)
4. Chari, K., Seshadri, S.: Demystifying Integration. Association for Computing Machinery. Communications of the ACM 47(7), 59 (2004)
5. Goodhue, D.L., Wybo, M.D., Kirsch, L.J.: The Impact of Data Integration on the Costs and Benefits of Information Systems. MIS Quarterly 16(3), 293 (1992)
6. Hanseth, O., Ciborra, C.U., Braa, K.: The Control Devolution ERP and the Side-effects of Globalization. The Data Base for Advances in Informatin Systems 32(4), 34–46 (2001)
7. Kallinikos, J.: Farewell to Constructivism: Technology and Context-Embedded Action. In: The Social Study of IT (2004)
8. Pollock, N., Cornford, J.: Customising industry standard computer systems for universities: ERP systems and the university as a 'unique' organisation. Information Technology & People 17(1), 31–52 (2004)
9. Singletary, L.A.: Applications Integration: Is it Always Desirable? In: Proceedings of the Proceedings of the 37th Annual Hawaii International Conference on System Sciences (HICSS 2004) - Track 8, vol. 8, p. 80265.1. IEEE Computer Society, Los Alamitos (2004)
10. Hanseth, O., Ciborra, C. (eds.): Risk, complexity and ICT. Edward Elgar Publishing, London (2007)
11. Perrow, C.: Normal accidents: Living with high-risk technologies, vol. X, p. 451. Princeton University Press, Princeton (1999)
12. Law, J.: Ladbroke Grove, or How to Think About Failing Systems (2003), http://www.lancs.ac.uk/fass/sociology/papers/law-ladbroke-grove-failing-systems.pdf
13. Shapin, S.: A Social History of Truth: Civility and Science in Seventeenth-Century England. Science and Its Conceptual Foundations. University of Chicago Press, Chicago (1995)
14. Boland Jr., R.J., Tenkasi, R.V.: Perspective making and perspective taking in communities of knowing. Organization Science 6(4), 350 (1995)
15. Cicourel, A.V.: The integration of distributed knowledge in collaborative medical diagnosis. In: Intellectual Teamwork: Social and Technological Foundations of Cooperative Work, pp. 221–242. L. Erlbaum Associates Inc., Mahwah (1990)
16. Walsham, G.: Doing interpretive research. European Journal of Information Systems 15(3), 320 (2006)
17. Klein, H.K., Myers, M.D.: A Set of Principles for Conducting and Evaluating Interpretive Field Studies in Information Systems. MIS Quarterly 23(1), 67–93 (1999)
18. Eisenhardt, K.: Building Theories from Case Study Research. Academy of Management Review 14(4), 532–551 (1989)
19. Maanen, J.V.: Tales of the Field, vol. xvi, p. 173. The University of Chicago Press, Chicago (1988)

20. Porter, T.M.: Trust in numbers: the pursuit of objectivity in science and public life, vol. xiv, p. 310. Princeton University Press, Princeton (1995)
21. Perin, C.: Shouldering Risks: The Culture of Control in the Nuclear Power Industry, p. 352. Princeton University Press, Princeton (2004)
22. Perby, M.-L.: Computerization and Skill in Local Weather Forecasting. In: Göranzon, B., Josefson, I. (eds.) Knowledge, Skill and Artificial Intelligence, pp. 39–52. Springer, Heidelberg (1988)

Changing Nature of Best Practices in eHealth

Janne Lahtiranta

University of Turku, School of Economics, FI-20014 Turku, Finland
janne.lahtiranta@it.utu.fi

Abstract. Best practices have been used in the health care sector for a long time. These practices that aim for delivering high quality care are commonly associated with clinical use by health care professionals. However, over time these practices have found their way to adjacent spheres of operation outside clinical practice (such as, nutrition, rehabilitation, etc.). Computerization of these practices and introducing them to the field of Electronic Health Care (eHealth) as an integral part of intelligent systems, such as Decision Support Systems (DSSs) is not a trivial or a straightforward matter. In the health care setting, issues such as clinical freedom, ethics, legislation and even the 'all-encompassing' nature of the work (i.e. providing care) creates unique challenges that need addressing prior to introducing computerized practices into the health care processes. Another aspect of consequence that has recently risen is the consumer-centricity or consumerism that changes the balance between the health care professionals and the patients in terms of decision making. This article looks into this shift and on its artifacts; the Patient Decision Support Systems (PDSSs). In the light of these, the primary question is: what kind of impact these artifacts potentially have on the patient's decision making.

Keywords: eHealth, Health Information Systems, Decision Support Systems, Electronic Health Records.

1 Introduction

Use of generally-accepted methods, processes and techniques (i.e. best practices) in order to increase operational effectiveness has become a preferred way of conducting business in the industry. Particularly, in manufacturing and supply chain management, the idea of doing things 'better than before' by adopting operations models from other organizations, and even from other lines of industry, has gained a strong foothold. The idea is not novel in the field of health care where best practices have been used in patient care for decades in the form of algorithms, guidelines, protocols, etc. that commonly base on the evidence-based medicine (c.f. [1], p. 1122). The term "evidence-based medicine" refers to the use of best available information that has been systemically reviewed in the clinical decision making. While the term has been coined in 1980s (ibid.), authors such as Sackett et al. [2] track philosophical origins of evidence-based medicine all the way back to "mid-19th century Paris and earlier" (ibid., p. 71).

What has changed over time in the health care sector is that best practices have become more multiform, originating from other sources besides reviews of evidence-based

H. Salmela and A. Sell (Eds.): SCIS 2011, LNBIP 86, pp. 84–97, 2011.

medicine, and they are applied throughout the sector, from physical activity of elderly people to disease prevention (c.f. [3], [4]). These practices are today so diverse that companies such as Pharmexx Nordic have created a service called Nurse Adviser[1], where the use of different practices is tutored to health care professionals. Different best practices have also found their way to homes of the patients, for example, in the context of diabetes self-management (c.f. [5]).

In similar fashion to other lines of industry, best practices in health care have found a new form in Information and Communication Technology (ICT). Different practices are computerized and embedded into different information systems. These systems are used by health care professionals in their daily work and by patients in their own care, and that of their close ones (e.g., children or elderly parents). From the perspective of the health care professionals, commonly used systems in this context are different intelligent systems, such as Clinical Decision Support Systems (CDSSs) and Diagnosis Decision Support Systems (DDSSs). Example solutions include: POEMS, a postoperative care decision support system and SETH, a clinical toxicology advisor [6].

From the patient's perspective, the computerized practices are customarily embedded into different Personal Health Record systems (PHRs), Patient Decision Support Systems (PDSSs) and Internet sites that are used to support patients in their health endeavors (c.f. [7]). These kinds of solutions are used, amongst others, in interactive patient guidance, such as in prostate cancer screening (c.f. [8]).

Intelligent systems, in particular knowledge-driven DSSs that facilitate adherence to best practices in their operation (cf. [6], p. 32) have so far been primarily used by health care professionals. However, there are some examples that such system are gaining foothold amongst consumers as well. For example, service providers like WebMD[2] have created a PDSS called "Symptom Checker" that supports patient's decision making when faced with different treatment options. In addition, WebMD offers different interactive tools, such as one for analyzing whether one's lifestyle adheres to the principles of diabetes control. As an example of a different PDSS, Segal & Shahar [9] present a web-based solution called the PANDEX. The system, which applies Bayesian probabilistic model in the decision support rationales, is used in the domain of prenatal testing. The system is intended for the health care professionals as well as for the patients in the spirit of shared decision making.

It appears that these kinds of consumer-centric intelligent systems that base on varying degrees to best practices are becoming more and more widely used in the field of eHealth. These kinds of systems create acute challenges to the traditional patient-physician relationship, placing patients more in charge of their health outcomes. In the following, the significance of computerized practices is investigated primarily from the perspective of the patient; what kind of impact these practices potentially have on a) the individual's decision making and b) the relationship with the health care professional. Looking into these questions now is of the essence in order to understand how to help the patients of the near-future to make better health related decisions with the aid of intelligent systems.

The findings in this article base on a 2-year national level project called "MyWellbeing"[3] where an artifact called "*the Coper*" was conceptualized. Aim of the

---

[1] http://www.pharmexx.se/en/Nurse-Advisers/ (accessed: 25.3.2011)
[2] http://www.webmd.com (accessed: 25.3.2011)
[3] http://omahyvinvointi.utu.fi/index.php?id=70 (accessed: 25.3.2011)

project was to look into the changing electronic service landscape and analyze what kind of means are required in order to promote the citizen into the center of the (electronic) services. In the field of electronic health care services, one of the identified mechanisms was supporting individual's autonomy with the use of DSSs and automated scripts. The primary means used in the concept development were use scenarios, prototypes and focus groups in which feedback on the use of the prototypes was collected directly from the citizens.

2   Best Practices in Health Care

Enrico Coiera ([6], pp. 401) defines a (clinical) guideline as "an agreed set of steps to be taken in the management of a clinical condition". These kinds of established guidelines are used particularly in routine clinical practice, for example, when a particular set of findings is investigated in a patient, or when a certain disease, or some other (commonly occurring) ailment is encountered.

Clinical guidelines, such as Current Care Guidelines (CCGs) in Finland or Evidence-Based Medicine Guidelines (EBM Guidelines) globally, are based on established and proven practices reflecting a rational and scientific view on health care delivery. In the spirit of evidence-based medicine, the purpose of the guidelines is to provide a "synthesis of the best available research evidence" ([10], p. 110) on issues such as prevention, diagnosis, prognosis and therapy. Clinical guidelines range from very strict to suggestive advice and they can be found in almost every area of health care delivery (research, self-care, education, etc.).

When a guideline, a phenomenon of evidence-based medicine, is defined in a form of concrete set of steps with a specific course of action in mind, an alternative term *protocol* is sometimes used. While a guideline, as its name states, emphasizes guidance and even advisory nature of practice, a protocol is typically more formally and precisely defined. Protocols often contain a more refined set of instructions, or even rules, to be executed and monitored in a controlled fashion. In the context of decision support, these protocols are sometimes realized using a protocol representation language (such as Asbru) or *pseudocode* (see example in the figure 1):

```
plan Hyperbilirubinemia
        intentions
                avoid intermediate-state: (bilirubin = transfusion)
conditions
        abort-condition: (possibility-of-hemolytic-disease = yes)
plan-body type = unordered, wait-for-optional-subplans = yes
wait-for Diagnostics-and-Treatment-hyperbilirubinemia
        Check-for-rapid-TSB-increase
        Check-for-jaundice-after-2-weeks
        Check-for-jaundice-after-3-weeks
        Diagnostics-and-Treatment-hyperbilirubinemia
```

Fig. 1. Portion of Asbru protocol for the Management of Hyperbilirubinemia in the Healthy Term Newborn [11]

Orient et al used a decision rule to evaluate men with abdominal pain. The rule was slightly modified by one developed by Wasson et al. The authors are from the University of Arizona.

The decision rule was developed in ambulatory men from the VA System.

Parameters:
(1) pain duration
(2) epigastric pain
(3) age
(4) pain features
(5) effect of pain on sleep
(6) abdominal and pelvic physical examination findings
(7) occult blood in stool
(8) vomiting
(9) weight loss
(10) past history

Parameter	Finding	Points
pain duration	pain for at least 6 months, OR at least 10 previous occurrence of pain	-3
	pain for less than 6 months AND less than 10 previous episodes	0
Epigastric pain and tenderness	only finding	-2
	absent or other findings present	0
Age	>= 60 years of age	+4
	< 60 years of age	0
pain features	pain is constant OR pain is unrelieved by food or medication	+4
	pain inconstant AND relieved by food or medication	0
pain has affected sleep	yes	+3
	no	0
abdominal and pelvic exam findings	mass, rigidity, rebound, distention, absent bowel sounds or an abnormal liver	+3
	negative examination	0
stool testing for occult blood	positive	+3
	negative	0
Vomiting since pain began	yes	+2
	no	0
change in weight	unintentional weight loss >= 10 pounds	+1
	weight gain or no change or unintentional weight loss < 10 pounds or intentional loss	0
History	cancer, diverticular disease, pancreatitis, gallstones, or inflammatory bowel disease	+6
	negative history	0

where:
   Removal of the gallbladder would seem to reduce the significance of a history of gallbladder disease.
   The time interval for weight loss is unspecified.

total score =
= SUM(points for all parameters) - 5

Interpretation:
   A score < 0 indicates a low likelihood of serious disease.

Limitations:
   Patients with peptic ulcer disease may be classified as low risk.
   Diseases outside of the abdomen and pelvis may present with abdominal pain. The score may indicate a low risk for
      serious abdominal disease yet the patient have a serious disease elsewhere.

Fig. 2. Decision rule of Orient et al. for men with abdominal pain. Copyright (c) 2010, Institute for Algorithmic Medicine, Houston, TX, USA. All rights reserved.

An *algorithm*, however, can be seen as a slightly different concept. While a protocol defines steps to be taken in order to achieve a specific goal, an algorithm is commonly a more mathematical or mechanistic; a step towards more computerized set of rules. Examples of algorithms in the health care setting include: Body Mass Index (BMI) calculator and a binary decision tree for defining etiology of a chest pain [12]. In literature, the concepts of algorithm and protocol overlap. For example,

Strauss ([13], p. 35) uses in her article a combination of *protocol algorithm* to describe a method for sepsis treatment. An illustrative example of an algorithm from the Medical Algorithms project[4] is presented in the figure 2.

Making a distinction between algorithms, protocols and guidelines is not always easy. While some of the guidelines can be extremely detailed, there are protocols that are defined on a much more abstract level. Guidelines, protocols and algorithms may also overlap, for example when a reference to one is made from another (from guideline to protocol, from algorithm to protocol, and so on).

One kind of a super-structure for guidelines, protocols and even algorithms in health care setting is an (Integrated) Care Pathway. These pathways define a general outline of anticipated care, placed within a specific timeframe such as a patient visit (c.f. [14]). The pathways are in place in order to help health care professionals and patients to move through the clinical experience to a positive outcome. When Care Pathways are applied, there is often more room for clinical freedom than with protocols and algorithms that can be seen as ones representing a more mechanistic view on care (figure 3).

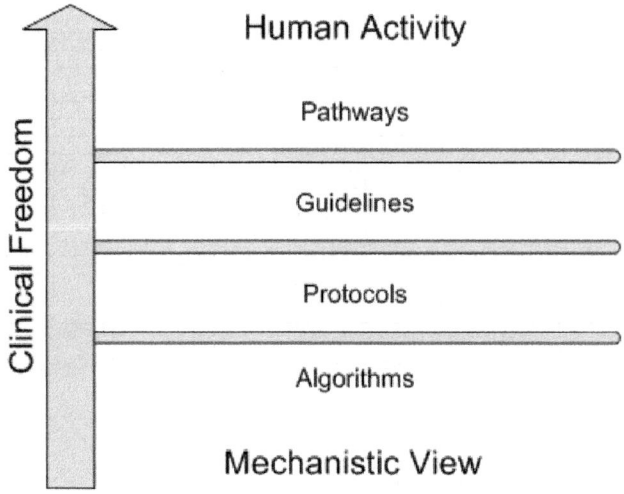

Fig. 3. Interpretation: pathways, guidelines, protocols and algorithms

Clinical freedom (or clinical autonomy) is a term that signifies health care professional's autonomy and control over one's decisions and work activities (on the level of practice) for the benefit of a patient [15]. The term is closely linked with concepts like clinical judgment and experience, creating an image of a practically wise doctor who provides advice and treatment "on the basis of intuition, experience, and attention to particulars" [16]. Clinical freedom can also be seen as a metaphor for situation awareness and even for insight; viewpoints which can be both lacking in the narrower scope of more mechanistic alternatives. Partially from this viewpoint, there

---

[4] http://www.medal.org (accessed: 25.3.2011).

has been some debate for and against protocols and evidence-based medicine in general (cf. [17], [15], p. 129). While protocols and guidelines can be considered to some extent as means of bureaucracy and control, similarly to best practices in other lines of business, they are widely used tools that bring evidence into medical practice, complementing individualistic factors (and moral values) of different human actors on issues such as perceived quality, cultural characteristics and value-of-life.

Best practices in the form of different guidelines, protocols and algorithms to be used by the patients in their own care, or in that of their close ones, are also becoming a commonplace practice in the wake of different Personal Health Information Management (PHIM) solutions. For example, in the EBMeDS[5], the implemented medical scripts have three distinct target groups: physician, nurse and citizen. Purpose of this classification is to indicate to what degree the scripts are suitable for use by different group(s). In the case of the patients, the scripts could be used as an integral part of a PDSS or a PHR system; a solution that could support the use of published scripts, that often include medical terms and other domain specific jargon, by laypeople.

Customarily, all instructions provided to the patient are reviewed by the health care professional prior to their use in order to ensure their timeliness and applicability. In general, these instructions are gone through with the patient, for example, at the doctor's (or nurse's) appointment in order to ensure that the patients have understood how to employ them properly. Amongst others, the instructions may contain information on how to treat their ailments or diseases (incl. medication), how to prepare for an operation and what to do after an operation in order to ensure a better recovery (c.f. [18]).

Recently, in the clinical domain a viewpoint that emphasizes the role of the patient in the health care processes has emerged. The viewpoint focuses on the processes from the patient's point of view, highlighting issues such as potential problems and areas of improvement (cf. [19], [20]). Introduction of this viewpoint has also led into definition of different patient journey modeling endeavors, such as the adaptation of the Systems Development Life Cycle (SDLC) approach presented by Curry et al. [21].

Nowadays, health related instructions originate often from other sources than from face-to-face meetings with the health care professionals. Since more and more different personal health and medical monitoring devices are used in health care by patients themselves, information on the health outcomes from using such devices are provided on manufacturer's web pages as well. Similarly, Internet and different forms of social media (virtual communities, portals, etc.) have also claimed a strong position as a preferred source of patient instructions (c.f. [22], p. 397).

3   Consumer-Centric eHealth Solutions of Today

Technologically, during the last five years the ICT industry has provided individuals better tools for 'empowerment' in the context of health care and well-being, or means for controlling their health decisions and actions. Internet in itself has brought not just health related information, but also health care and well-being services to the grasp of

---

[5] http://www.mrex.fi/EBMeDS/ (accessed 27.4.2011).

the technology literate young. For example, Kaelber et al. [23] argue that approximately 70 million people in the United States alone have access to some form of PHR. Similar technological advance can be seen in the Europe as well since more and more EHR solutions are becoming accessible to citizens via Internet and new media. For example, in Finland a possibility to access one's public health records are implemented as a part of upcoming KanTa[6] services. At the same time the ICT service providers such as Google and Microsoft are implementing their own consumer-centric PHR solutions that can be used in personal health information management.

The motivations behind this kind of development are rather evident; while the ICT sector aims for new markets in the sector that has proven to be difficult to penetrate, the public health care sector strives to motivate individuals to take better care of themselves (and their relatives) in order to be able to better allocate their limited funding. The latter perspective has, for its part, given birth to a multi-layered phenomenon often referred as 'empowerment'. While the concept in the context of health care and well-being services is often seen as a synonym to 'self-service', it is actually connected to issues such as awareness, power, influence and autonomy (c.f. [24], [25]). Especially from this viewpoint, the narrow interpretation of the concept is rather troubling since it carries a notion that individuals are automatically *willing* to take the burden of their health management upon their shoulder.

While the consumer-centric PHR and EHR solutions of today give patients means for taking actively part in the health care processes, the current development of the solutions seems to imply that they *should* take more responsibility over their (incl. their families) health care and related information management. Somewhat similar paradigm change occurred on a smaller scale when the online banking (or Internet banking) was introduced around the 1980s. However, what is fundamentally different from information systems development perspective is that online banking is regulated; as is the case with the overall banking sector [26]. In health care sector, the online service providers are more diverse; for example, the myPHR[7] web site lists around 30 free and 60 for purchase online services that can be used for health services or health information management.

Partly due to this fragmentation of potential service providers and partly due to the imprecise nature of what can be regarded as 'health' or 'well-being', the electronic health care services are often heterogeneous by nature and provided by diversity of different service providers. From the best practices point of view, this means that controlling the source, validity and timeliness of the practice in question can be difficult. While in the 1970's and 1980's the individuals 'empowered' by the books of medicine or pharmaceutical drug guides, and so on, were able to make more or less accurate references to a printed, published and even reviewed sources, the 'empowered' individuals today often come to the doctor's office armed with miscellaneous prints from a wide variety of sources available online (c.f. [27]).

Continuing with the online banking metaphor, what we see in today's health care sector solutions is not just empowerment, or placing responsibility over one's health on the individuals themselves, but consumerism as well (cf. [28]). However, the

---

[6] https://www.kanta.fi/web/en/frontpage (accessed 27.4.2011).
[7] http://www.myphr.com/ (accessed 4.2.2011).

staggering first steps of consumerism we see in today's eHealth are far from those of online banking where transactions can be completed successfully, even on a global scale, with few simple mouse clicks.

4 Computerization of Best Practices in Health Care

Giving a computerized interpretation to a health care best practice (i.e. algorithm, protocol or guideline) is a challenge. It is rarely possible to translate health care practices into computer algorithms in such a way that they are universally applicable. Even with a simplest algorithm, there is a risk that when computerized and integrated into a DSS, it becomes too rigid and liming (cf. [29]). Furthermore, our unarticulated assumptions on the very nature of health create unique challenges to computerization; health is not a simple and precise science and patients rarely fit to any exact pattern or disease, but they present different stages of an illness, different combinations of symptoms, and they have different capabilities for recovery ([6], p. 184).

When written in a computerized format, or as computer programs, and embedded into intelligent systems such as DSSs, health care algorithms, protocols and guidelines become manifestations of industry's "best practices" much in a same way as in other lines of business, such as in manufacturing or in finance. However, at the same time the very aspects that differentiate health care from other lines of industry, especially those of manufacturing and assembly, are potentially "lost in the translation". For example, in the health care setting, professionals have a right and duty to employ clinical freedom in their judgment for the benefit of a patient ([15], p. 128). In the light of best practices, this can result in applying *in situ* practices instead of the *de facto* ones in order to engender clinician reflexivity.

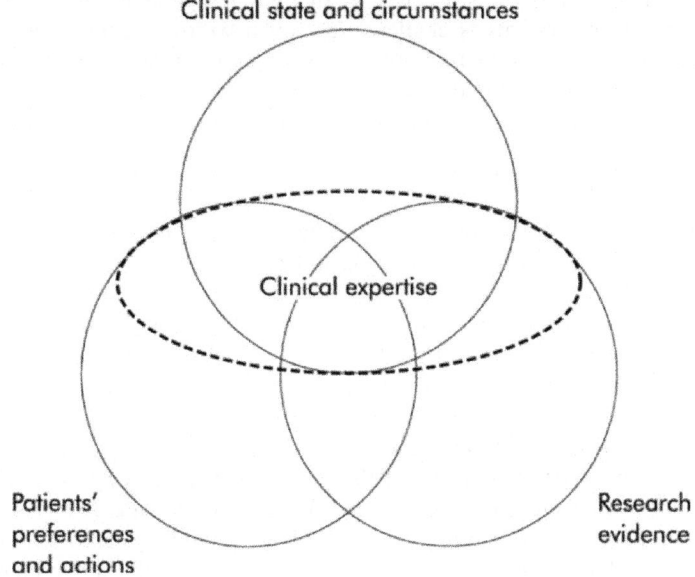

Fig. 4. An updated model for evidence-based clinical decisions ([30], p. 37)

For taking health care domain specific aspects such as clinical freedom, patient autonomy and preferences, and the current clinical state into account, Haynes, Devereaux & Guyatt [30] propose a new prescriptive model for evidence-based clinical decisions (figure 4).

Purpose of this reviewed model is to highlight the role of the individual practitioner in the decision making situation as an expert who can balance different factors (i.e. research evidence, patient preferences, etc.) in order to achieve a successful result that will satisfy the patient and the clinician (ibid., pp. 37-38).

Creating a computerized practice that would highlight the role of the individual practitioner, allowing a required degree of freedom for both, the health care professional and the patient, is by no means a trivial task. For example, if the computerized best practice does not give room for a reasonable use of *in situ* practices, there is a risk of conflict that would potentially impede the workflow of the patient. In the academic literature, Bates et al. ([29], p. 525) emphasize the need for creating this kind of balance between the physician's workflow and the use of DSSs.

A similar conflict may occur if the computerized practice violates the user's individualistic values, or those that can be regarded as a cultural norm, potentially resulting in a total patient non-adherence. In the changing world of today where cultural background of a patient cannot be determined on the basis of one's residence or country of origin, the significance of clinical expertise (and social skills) are further emphasized. In order to avoid conflicts in the patient-physician relationship, the clinician, or another person with sufficient clinical expertise, needs to act in a role of a *facilitator*, interpreting different guidelines and adapting to the current situation of the individual. These kinds of interpretive viewpoints to facilitation in health care setting are depicted in Harvey, et al. [31], where the activities of the facilitator categorized as 'enabling others' are closest to the ones pursued here (ibid., p. 581-582).

Bringing these kinds of 'soft' aspects that are inseparable part of care into the different intelligent systems is challenging – even with the technology of the near-future. Replacing human factor with 'an automaton' requires implementation of human characteristics such as care and compassion, even camaraderie into the solutions. At the moment, it seems unforeseeable that such will become available.

Patient-physician relationship

Regardless of the recent advances and the future trends in the consumer-centricity, and in the patient-centered medicine, the relationship between the patient and the physician has been traditionally characterized as a *paternalistic* one. A paternalistic relationship bases on trust and as such it is assumed that the physician is a beneficent one ([32], p. 41). In this kind of relationship, the physician controls the health care process and has a moral authority and discretion [33]. In a paternalistic relationship the patient may have little room for affecting on how the actual care is provided.

Another metaphor used by Beisecker & Beisecker [32] for a relationship is *consumerism* in which it is assumed that the doctor is self-centered (ibid., p. 41). Unlike in a paternalistic relationship, consumerism can be regarded as a relationship where the patient has equal power, or even more, as the physician. In consumerism trust is replaced with accountability and individual's health care preferences may override the principles and the best practices of a good medical practice.

Scott & Lenert [34] add to the discussion a metaphor of a *deliberative* patient-physician relationship. In this kind of relationship, the physician abandons objectivity and strives to influence patient's values and beliefs on health outcomes. In this kind of relationship, the physician acts as a teacher or as a friend who may suggest to the patient what avenues to pursue in one's care. As a comparison, Scott & Lenert (ibid.) also present a *collaborative* relationship where the physician attempts to elicit patient's values and actively assists in selecting the most appropriate care from one's viewpoint.

This kind of collaborative patient-physician relationship is close to an *informed* one where the physician acts as a domain expert and has a duty to provide all the necessary facts to the patient (ibid., p. 785). The primary difference between these two relationship metaphors is the active role of the physician. Unlike in the informed relationship, the collaborative metaphor highlights the physician's role in the process of discovering patient's individualistic values and their significance to the health related decisions.

Patient decision making

When a best practice is computerized, it can become more mechanistic; void of 'soft' aspects such as care, compassion and values of life. As such, when integrated into a PDSS, the practice can be seen as *inherently* deliberative, steering individual's health related decisions without objectivity or elicitation of individual's preferences. Furthermore, our tendency to treat computers and new technologies as real people and objects of trust [35] may change our perception about the artifact, placing it into a paternalistic position as well. In theory, this may lead to a situation in which we place our trust on the artifact as we would on an actual physician.

In contrast to physicians, patients make health related decisions relatively infrequently. Most of the decisions are made with a little or no preparation or repetition. In addition, patient decisions are often guided by misconceptions, such as folklore, prior beliefs and anecdotal knowledge [36]. In the health care setting, individuals are also prone to emotional misinterpretations, for example when facing difficult medical decisions, or decisions that will have an effect to their perceived quality of life [37].

Rooting out potential negative effects of patient's emotions, misinterpretations and lack of clinical knowledge is not a trivial task. In a face-to-face situation individual practitioners may employ different strategies, such as taking advantage of time in order to allow patient's strong emotions to dissipate ([36], p. 180-181). In the case of intelligent systems, employing these kinds of strategies that require social acumen, and balancing human factors against best practices that base on hard realities of the evidence-based medicine, is challenging.

5 Recommendations

Health care is a knowledge intensive field and in its core is the individual. The individual is not always the same; in the same role, and the situation in which best practices are to be applied varies significantly. Cultural aspects, personal values and preferences, experience of the attending physician, etc. have an impact on the situation into which the practice is applied. Similarly, the practice itself and the level of detail it encloses, changes the way it is to be applied. When a best practice is computerized and integrated into an intelligent system such as PDSS, a special focus on its *applicability* should be paid.

As established, in any clinical encounter achieving a comprehensive picture of the individual's current health status is of the essence. The health care professionals typically have different information sources at their disposal (incl. the patient), and they may employ different strategies when creating a hypothesis on the course of action to follow. In the case of intelligent systems, these functions are often lacking; there is no health care professional who verifies the result (or the recommendation) provided by the artifact. In addition, the decision support rationale of the artifact may be vague to the user who often acquires the result by following a simple decision path, such as yes/no choices or stepwise definition of the current ailment (e.g. location, symptom, severity, etc.).

Basically, the defined decision path and the underlying interaction mechanism also define the degree of freedom the patient has. Especially in the case of more mechanistic practices there is rarely room for vagueness or interpretation and the patient choice is limited to the available options they must use in order to acquire a result from the artifact. Furthermore, there are rarely any kinds of mechanisms in place that ensure patient adherence. On the practical level, the patients may create their own adaptations of the practices, solely on the basis of their preferences, beliefs and (anecdotal) knowledge.

In order to help patients to make better health related decisions by using intelligent systems, *intervention* and *mediation* mechanisms should be implemented into the intelligent systems that help in ensuring applicability of the computerized best practice. Effectively, this means that if misinterpretation of the results may potentially lead to negative health effects, the system should discontinue its analysis and help the individual to seek professional help who could properly analyze the current situation.

This kind of functionality requires role-based implementation. As in the case of the EBMeDS[8] database, the implemented medical scripts have been categorized by three distinct target groups in order to indicate to what degree the scripts are suitable for different user groups. With a functional role-based implementation, the intelligent systems could be programmed to break out of their decision making routines when a potential health risk to a 'non-conforming' user group emerges.

Understanding in which role the decision support system and the underlying best practice(s) are used could also be of assistance when additional mediation mechanisms are implemented. For example, in the case of a citizen who is often a layperson in terms of used vocabulary and concepts, a 'translated' version void of domain specific jargon could be provided instead. However, this alone is not a sufficient measure for ensuring that individuals understand what kinds of artifacts and information they are using in health related decision making.

In addition to providing 'translated' versions of intelligent systems and best practices, individuals' health literacy skills should be improved. Health literacy which refers to "citizen's ability to recognize their needs for health information, to search for that information, to assess the validity of the information gained, and to apply that

---

[8] http://www.mrex.fi/EBMeDS/

information" ([38], p. 242), should be identified as one of the key arts to be taught already in the elementary schools, for example as an integral part of health education classes.

6 Conclusions

In terms of social interaction, there is no substitute for a face-to-face meeting and the traditional patient-physician interaction. No matter how advanced the employed intelligent systems are there are no mechanisms in place that can carry the emotional undertones of the physical world. Similarly, the 'soft' aspects that are inseparable part of care are, as a rule, missing from the intelligent systems.

It can be argued that intelligent systems potentially change individual's perceptions about the patient-physician relationship and the underlying balance of power therefore affecting individual's decision making. At least in theory, issues such as inherently deliberative decision support mechanisms and misplaced trust shift patient's expectations on the health outcomes. However, computerized best practices that are integrated into different intelligent systems *are* a part of today's health care landscape; they can be seen as aids that support patient's decision making processes and help in bridging the gap between the clinical domain and expertise, and the laypeople's beliefs, fears and (anecdotal) knowledge. In this lies the fundamental question: to what degree we should encourage people to use such systems in their own 'diagnoses'?

A partial answer to this question lies within implementing mechanisms that can be used in creating artifacts that fit better for the purpose in terms of individual's current clinical state and values, consequently avoiding the pitfall associated with the inherently deliberative decision support mechanisms. From this perspective, what we need can be seen as *personalized* patient decision support and mediation; intelligent systems with the soft touch of a human expert.

References

1. Rosenberg, W., Donald, A.: Evidence based medicine: an approach to clinical problem-solving. BMJ 310, 1122–1126 (1995)
2. Sackett, D.L., Rosenberg, W.M., Gray, J.A., Haynes, R.B., Richardson, W.S.: Evidence Based Medicine: What it is and What it isn't. BMJ 312, 71–72 (1996)
3. Cress, M.E., Buchner, D.M., Prohaska, T., Rimmer, J., Brown, M., Macera, C., DePietro, L., Chodzko-Zajko, W.: Best practices for physical activity programs and behavior counseling in older adult populations. Eur. Rev. Aging Phys. Act. 3(1), 34–42 (2006)
4. Cameron, R., Jolin, M.A., Walker, R., McDermott, N., Gough, M.: Linking Science and practice: toward a system for enabling communities to adopt best practices for chronic disease prevention. Health Promot. Pract. 2(1), 35–42 (2001)
5. Mensing, C., Boucher, J., Cypress, M., Weinger, K., Mulchamy, K., Barta, P., Hosey, G., Kopher, W., Lasichak, A., Lamb, B., Mangan, M., Norman, J., Tanja, J., Yauk, L., Wisdom, K., Adams, C.: National standards for diabetes self-management education. Diabetes Care 25(1), 140–147 (2002)
6. Coiera, E.: Guide to Health Informatics, 2nd edn. Arnold, London (2003)

7. O'Connor, A., Wennberg, J.E., Legare, F., Llewellyn-Thomas, H.A., Moulton, B.W., Sepucha, K.R., Sodano, A.G., King, J.S.: Toward the 'tipping point': decision aids and informed patient choise. Health Aff. (Millwood) 26(3), 716–725 (2007)
8. Frosch, D.L., Bhatnagar, V., Tally, S., Hamori, C.J., Kaplan, R.M.: Internet patient decision support - a randomized controlled trial comparing alternative approaches for men considering prostate cancer screening. Arch. Intern. Med. 168(4), 363–369 (2008)
9. Segal, I., Shahar, Y.: A Distributed System for Support and Explanation of Shared Decision-Making in the Prenatal Testing Domain. JBI (2008)
10. Mead, P.: Clinical Guidelines: Promoting Clinical Effectiveness or a Professional Minefield? J. Adv. Nurs. 31(1), 110–116 (2000)
11. Roomans, H., Berger, G., Marcos, M., ten Teije, A., Seyfang, A., van Harmelen, F.: Asbru Protocol for the Management of Hyperbilirubinemia in the Healthy Term Newborn. Technical Report IR-495. Vrije Universiteit Amsterdam (2002), http://www.protocure.org/old/Protocols/jaundice-protocolAug28.pdf
12. Focsa, M.: EHR Integration of Medical Algorithms. In: Reichert, A., Mihalas, G., Stoicu-Tividar, L., Schulz, S., Engelbrecht, R. (eds.) Integrating Biomedical Information: From eCell to ePatient - Proceedings of the European Federation for Medical Informatics Special Topic Conference, pp. 392–394 (2006)
13. Strauss, M.P.: A New Approach to an Old Foe: Implementation of an Early Goal-Directed Sepsis Treatment Protocol. JEN 31(1), 34–38 (2005)
14. Middleton, S., Barnett, J., Reeves, D.: What is an integrated care pathway. What is...? Series, vol. 3(3). Hayward Group Plc., U.K. (2001)
15. Hampton, J.R.: Evidence-based medicine, practice variations and clinical freedom. J. Eval. Clin. Pract. 3(2), 123–131 (1997)
16. Parker, M.: False dichotomies: EBM, clinical freedom, and the art of medicine. JME; Medical Humanities 31, 23–30 (2005)
17. Berg, M.: Problems and Promises of the Protocol. Soc. Sci. Med. 44, 1081–1088 (1997)
18. Arnell, T.: Preopearative patient instructions. The Sages Manual, Part 1, 20–24 (2006)
19. Trebble, T.M., Hansi, N., Hydes, T., Smith, M.A., Baker, M.: Process mapping the patient journey through health care: an introduction. BMJ 341, 341–401 (2010)
20. Howard, P., Jonkers-Schuitema, C., Furniss, L., Kyle, U., Muehlebach, S., Ödlund-Olin, A., Page, M., Wheatley, C.: Managing the patient journey through enteral nutritional care. Am. J. Clin. Nutr. 25, 187–195 (2006)
21. Curry, J.M., McGregor, C., Tracy, S.: A Systems Development Life Cycle Approac to Patient Journey Modeling Projects. In: Kuhn, K.A., Warren, J.R., Leong, T. (eds.) MEDINFO 2007: Proceedings of the 12th World Congress on Health (Medical) Informatics: Building Sustainable Health Systems. IOS Press, Amsterdam (2007)
22. Sillence, E., Briggs, P., Harris, P., Fishwick, L.: Going online for health advice: changes in usage and trust practices over the last five years. Interact. Comput. 19, 397–406 (2007)
23. Kaelber, D.C., Jha, A.K., Johnston, D., Middleton, B., Bates, D.W.: A Research Agenda for Personal Health Records (PHRs). JAMIA 15(6), 729–736 (2008)
24. Rappaport, J.: Term of empowerment/exemplars of prevention: toward a theory of community psychology. Am. J. Commun. Psychol. 15(2), 121–148 (1987)
25. Anderson, R.M., Funnell, M.M.: Patient empowerment: myths and misconceptions. Patient Educ. Couns. 79, 277–282 (2010)
26. Corvoisier, S., Gropp, R.: Contestability, Technology and Banking. In: EFA 2002 Berlin Meetings Presented Paper (2001)

27. Akekar, S.M., Bichile, L.S.: Doctor patient relationship: changing dynamics in the information age. J. Postgrad. Med. 50(2), 120–122 (2004)
28. Robinson, J.C.: Managed consumerism in health care. Health Aff. (Millwood) 24(6), 1478–1489 (2005)
29. Bates, D.W., Kuperman, G.J., Wang, S., Gandhi, T., Kittler, A., Volk, L., Spurr, C., Khorasani, R., Tanasijevic, M., Middleton, B.: Ten Commandments for Effective Clinical Decision Support: Making the Practice of Evidence-based Medicine a Reality. JAMIA 10(6), 523–530 (2003)
30. Haynes, R.B., Deveraux, P.J., Guyatt, G.H.: Clinical expertise in the era of evidence-based medicine and patient choice. EBM 7(2), 28–36 (2002)
31. Harvey, G., Loftus-Hills, A., Rycroft-Malone, J., Titchen, A., Kitson, A., McCormack, B., Seers, K.: Getting evidence into practice: the role and function of facilitation. J. Adv. Nurs. 37(6), 577–588 (2002)
32. Beisecker, A.E., Beisecker, T.D.: Using Metaphors to Characterize Doctor-Patient Relationships: Paternalism Versus Consumerism. Health Commun. 5(1), 41–58 (1993)
33. Childress, J.F., Siegler, M.: Metaphors and Models of Doctor-Patient Relationships: Their Implications for Autonomy. Theor. Med. 5(1), 17–30 (1984)
34. Scott, G.C., Lenert, L.A.: What is the next step in patient decision support. In: Proceedings of the AMIA Symposium 2000, pp. 784–788 (2000)
35. Reeves, B., Nass, C.: The Media Equation: How People Treat Computers, Television, and the New Media Like Real People and Places. Cambridge University Press, New York (1996)
36. Ubel, P.A.: Patient Decision Making. In: Chang, A.E., Ganz, P.A., Hayes, D.F., Kinsella, T.J., Pass, H.I., Schiller, J.H., Stone, R.M., Strecher, V. (eds.) Oncology: an Evidence-Based Approach. Section One, pp. 177–183. Springer, U.S. (2006)
37. Ubel, P.A., Loewenstein, G., Jepson, C.: Whose quality of life? A commentary exploring discrepancies between health state evaluations of patients and the general public. QLR 12, 599–607 (2003)
38. Ek, S.: Information mastering as a pathway to social equity in health. In: Suomi, R., Apiainen, S. (eds.) Promoting Health in Urban Living (WIS 2008), vol. 49, pp. 241–249. TUCS General Publication (August 2008)

Planning for Inter-Organizational Information Systems in Practice

Marko Mäkipää

University of Tampere, Kanslerinrinne 1,
33100 Tampere, Finland
marko.makipaa@uta.fi

Abstract. Globally distributed production and high proportion of outsourcing have increased the need to orchestrate the key network participating to production of end-products. Information is driving the network operations and thus, significance of inter-organizational information systems supporting the cooperation is evident. In this study, the growing phenomenon of Planning for Inter-Organizational Information Systems (PIOS) is examined with multiple case study approach. Empirical evidence is collected from three large multinational manufacturing corporations and their IOS planning practices to identify critical planning characteristics perceived by practitioners. Results of a two-round evaluation are presented as well as general observations of companies' PIOS practices.

Keywords: Planning, Inter-Organizational Information Systems, Inter-Organizational Relationships, critical success factors, multiple case study.

1 Introduction

Cooperative inter-organizational relationships (IORs) have been acknowledged to have a significant role in formation of companies' competitiveness [1]. The continuing trend in business to concentrate on core competencies [2] and strategic outsourcing [3], boomed in the 1990's, has created inter-organizational dependencies between multiple parties in companies' business networks. Deep distribution of work can increase uncertainty between different performers. In order to reduce uncertainty and inefficiency among multiple actors the network partners have to cooperate to enable coordinated action.

Cooperative business relationships, just like any organizational arrangement, need tools for handling information flows efficiently and effectively. Business partners need information for various purposes such as transactions, product information, stock levels, availability, collaborative planning, coordination, process measurement, and decision-making. Information exchange is unquestionably critical in the operations of all business partnerships and thus, so are inter-organizational information systems (IOS) developed to handle these information flows.

Improving Information Systems Planning (ISP) has been rated as a top issue in Information Systems [4], [5]. Current methods and methodologies are criticized being to heavy and complex or lacking sufficient guidelines for developing effective IS plan [6].

H. Salmela and A. Sell (Eds.): SCIS 2011, LNBIP 86, pp. 98–111, 2011.

Also, their focus is on organizational rather than inter-organizational context. Cooperative business relationships, long-term partnerships and strategic alliances place new challenges for efficient and effective ISP in inter-organizational arrangements.

As an emerging research stream the extant literature provides only little insight and guidance on how to conduct Planning for Inter-Organizational Information Systems (PIOS) and how to help cooperative business networks to identify information exchange opportunities to improve efficiency and effectiveness. Yet, the use of different kinds of IOSs has been reported widely, e.g. supply chain systems [7], Electronic Data Interchange [8], Internet EDI [9] and B2B marketplaces [10]. Thus, it seems that the practice of PIOS is expansive but theory lacks behind.

In this paper this shortcoming is tackled from the perspective of large global manufacturers. Manufacturing has witnessed a strong division of labor while multinational companies (MNCs) are constantly building new or moving old production sites to more attractive locations throughout the globe and creating global networks of production units. Combining global and local suppliers require smart sourcing decisions and identification of key network partners. Also, management of large number of supplier relationships requires systematic processes, automation of activities and cooperative relationships.

The research questions studied were: 1) How planning for inter-organizational systems is practiced in cooperative inter-organizational relationships and 2) What planning characteristics practitioners identify for successful planning process of inter-organizational systems. Earlier studies have suggested that IOSs should be studied from a point-of-view of a) adoption studies, b) governance studies, and c) consequences studies [11]. Planning and design activities are not yet detected as an important part of IOS studies although all IOSs are planned and designed before implementation, use and consequences. Also, usually IOS involves integration of two or more information systems of two or more partners, rather than adopting a ready made package software application. Thus, this study focuses on IOS planning activities generally and critical success factors of PIOS especially.

Multiple case study method was selected for being able to extend knowledge beyond a single case [12]. Also, PIOS is still an emerging concept that requires conceptualization and development of context specific terminology. In this kind of research settings only qualitative research methods, such as multiple case study, can produce meaningful results. This is because in the interview situation researcher can interact with interviewees about subject area, used concepts can be explained and a common understanding can be created.

The rest of the paper is divided to sections as follows. In Section 2 the research setting and process of conducting interviews are described. The three cases are described in Section 3 and general results are presented in Section 4. The specific critical success factors identified by case companies are presented in Section 5. Section 6 concludes the paper with discussion.

2 Research Setting

2.1 Company Selection

Selected case companies are large global organizations with a long manufacturing tradition. A criterion for selection was that selected companies have manufacturing in more than one country and operations in more than one continent, true multinationals. These kinds of companies have complex internal structure with a lot of internal system linkages. Thus, it was expected that they have used accumulated experience of internal integration also to external relationships and have many inter-organizational information systems as well. As a result of decades of development on own core competencies and gradual outsourcing of other processes, many of these multinational manufacturing companies are in situation where even 60-80 percent of production costs accumulate from suppliers - outside the companies' direct control. In this situation the companies have a large amount of inter-organizational relationships that they are highly dependent from.

All interviewed companies are large multinational corporations. Large corporations as a study population were selected as they are usually forerunners in new management trends and disseminators of these ideas to their partner networks. All three companies are also very successful and thus, offer inspiration for managers and stimuli for further investigation [13].

Table 1. Characteristics of the interviewed companies

Company	GMM	BGM	GFIC
Industry	Machine construction	Machine construction	Forest Industry
Personnel	Over 10 000	Over 10 000	Over 10 000
Turnover	Over 1 billion euro	Over 1 billion euro	Over 1 billion euro
Production	In more than one continent	In more than one continent	In more than one continent
Operations	Around or over 50 countries	Around or over 50 countries	Around or over 50 countries

Among the all large global companies fulfilling the above criteria the interviewed three companies were selected because they all had previous contact with the researcher through different forms of research collaboration. Large MNCs are hard to persuade for interviews as they get so many invitations to participate different studies all the time. Previous collaboration and trusting relationship was considered essential in arrangement of the interviews.

2.2 Interviews

The study reported in this paper consists of 3 company visits, related documents and interviews with 7 IT and Business managers. Company interviews were conducted in 2007-2008. The interviewed managers were typically Chief Information Officers (CIOs), IT-managers and Business managers responsible for IOS planning activities. The companies selected the interviewees internally after the phone/email contact from the researcher. In addition, the researcher had background knowledge of the companies through previous joint research activities.

Contacts and interviewees represented one strategic business unit (SBU) or one process penetrating different SBUs in these large multinational corporations. This approach was seen necessarily for interviewees to have first hand contact with inter-organizational information systems planning. Yet, the interviewed persons had insights and experience from global systems and global planning processes and interviews can be considered representing the corporate practices.

After initial contact and agreement for interview, an outline of topics covered in interview were sent via email few days earlier for mental preparation. The interview reports were sent to interviewees to double-check for misinterpretations and correction of clear mistakes.

2.3 Interview Topics

A wide coverage of topics was planned to capture not only PIOS characteristics but also differences in company profiles leading to these differences. Approach was to move in interview from overall information to IS planning activities in general and finally to specific questions related to PIOS:

1. Company characteristics
2. IS-planning development and focus areas
3. PIOS planning characteristics
4. Critical Success Factors for PIOS

First, company characteristics give important background information to understand the reasons for different IT-planning characteristics and challenges. How the company positions itself today and where it's heading give an idea of current and forthcoming development challenges that might also entail IT-issues. Also, pre-hand acquaintance to company and its products e.g. through company website and a year book helps to understand the company and its characteristics better.

Second, how IS-planning overall is organized in the company tells how much of the planning is done locally and globally and what roles IT and Business representatives have. Also, if the focus of IS initiatives is heavily in certain area, e.g. in internal cost cutting or implementation of a new enterprise wide ERP-system, you can expect other areas getting less attention and resources at the time. Knowing what's up in the company, researcher can better understand and interpret the answers.

Third, the actual focus area, inter-organizational systems planning characteristics in the company; who participates, who is in charge and who covers the costs. And what is the approach to planning and how is it in congruence with general approach to partnership development. The prepared questions covered items like source of initiative, functions involved, focus of projects, level of organizational responsibility, IT/business leadership, sharing of costs, used planning methods and nature of planning.

Fourth, critical success factors (CSF) and other facilitating factors and barriers are widely studied in literature in different contexts [14], [15], [16]. As a definite part of IS research it is always interesting to know topic and context specific CSFs. What are the main reasons to withdraw from inter-organizational planning and what are the main critical success factors for PIOS to be successful?

3   Case Companies

3.1   Case 1: Global Machine Manufacturer, GMM (True Name Concealed)

GMM is a large global equipment and technology supplier for the global process industry. It has production in many continents and operations in around 50 countries.

GMM has global IT-department that is responsible for corporate wide IT-services and some commodity systems like accounting and HRM. Responsibility for other business applications is laid on different business units. Roles and responsibilities are divided so that GMM's global IT governance take a stand in many internal technology, data, and IT-management issues but not that much on actual planning for or business applications in use. What is globally defined is more like a policy than a detailed plan for business applications. Also, for IOSs IT governance defines only on what terms external links and views can be opened to internal systems, not what and with whom information is shared or how the planning is conducted.

All IT investments including IOSs are considered and evaluated as any other non-IT investment in the company and project planning has to follow general governance guidelines. Using monetary evaluation criteria, investments are divided to three classes: 1) maintenance and small development – few days' or few dozens of days' work, 2) bigger projects, and 3) strategic level projects. Earlier, there were a lot of local applications and responsibilities; now the tendency is toward global solutions and clear ownerships. However, a global planning methodology or a systematic practice for planning is only now under development and it will also take a stand how to plan IOSs.

Comparing to internal projects, IOS projects were considered to have some similarities and some differences. A large corporation has also a lot of internal projects connecting different business units and many challenges are similar than in IOS projects. However, in internal projects the evaluation of costs and benefits is much easier and allocation of costs to different business units can be much more detailed. Internally corporation also dictates a lot more, e.g. what technology will be used.

IOS planning with partners is considered to be mainly relational (e.g. based on trust and long-lasting cooperative relationship), although conditions of the actual solution follow more like a hierarchical planning approach. The size of a partner is a good indicator in this, if you have a logistics provider with 10 billion revenues and a half billion business unit negotiating about system changes, it is clear who does the changes… And a like, when a half billion business unit and a small workshop with few million revenues are discussing about system linkages it is easier to and also cheaper to change the smaller player's systems and practices.

3.2 Case 2: Global Building Mechanizer, GBM (True Name Concealed)

GBM is a large global supplier of mechanical equipment mainly to buildings world wide, one of the leading companies in its industry. It has manufacturing sites in many continents and operations in around 50 countries. In addition to internal complexity due to rapid growth through mergers and acquisitions, company has complex sourcing relationships with thousands of local and global suppliers.

During the interviews the GBM was in a process of global harmonization and standardization of IT practices. This process included definition of rules for different levels of IT initiatives and rules for project acceptance process. All project proposals are evaluated according to the same criteria by a global organization established to monitor global projects, e.g. even all small project proposals have to be evaluated if they could be extended to cover all units and only "compulsory" projects are allowed to be implemented locally. If a project is bigger or affects more than one unit it is automatically considered a global system requiring acceptance from global process owner or even from executive director's board. Generally, bigger projects require heavier acceptance procedure. With global control of IT-project proposals GBM is able to globally control priorization of projects, maximize resource allocation and control costs of IT-investments.

As a part of this harmonization development GBM had some time ago launched a global guidance for IT project management about which interviewed people had only had first experiences during the interview. There was no special guide for inter-organizational planning and thus, general planning guidance was used in IOS projects as well.

Generally IOS projects were initiated by both the company itself and its suppliers. Many times the source of initiation was yearly sourcing negotiations with suppliers. Typical situation for IOS planning is when the material prices became stagnant and the decrease in cost has to be sought from process improvement.

The GBM's cooperative practices include sharing order-book information with suppliers who deliver supplies according to yearly agreement. Also, a forecast package is delivered monthly on which suppliers can make their own conclusions and decide on their actions accordingly. The order book information includes references to PDM system from where the supplier can retrieve relevant CAD-designs and other product related information. However, the level of cooperation and required processes depend on the level of supplier; they are divided to local and global suppliers and to strategic and non-strategic suppliers.

3.3 Case: Global Forest Industry Company, GFIC (True Name Concealed)

GFIC is a large global supplier of wood and paper based products world wide, one of the leading companies in its industry. It has manufacturing sites in many continents and production facilities in around 50 countries. GFIC is operating in long lasting supplier partnerships, which is characteristic for the industry. In addition to suppliers, logistical partners are in important role in the total process and the logistical process is one of the main development areas.

IOS development in GFIC has concentrated on order-supply chain and on product information. Major part of IT development effort is around logistics and how product information follows the product all the way from suppliers to customers. Also, selected suppliers are given more responsibility for their supply activities (e.g. Vendor Managed Inventory). Company doesn't even try to manage the non-core business processes but seek to transfer the responsibility, to automate, and to standardize the process. However, GFIC has thousands of suppliers globally and IOS development activities comprise only fraction of them; GFIC is very cautious about when to build IOSs and with whom.

The IOS planning approach is mainly relational and concentrates on business development. Streamlining and redefining the business processes is the focus, but standardization and harmonization is done through information systems. The approach has to be largely relational, since relationships to suppliers, partners and customers are long and stable. Some cooperative development projects are done also with logistic organizations, but mostly logistic organizations are so big that company has to accommodate to their requirements on IOS projects. On the other hand, toward suppliers some requirements can be dictated when seeking for own operational benefits. Overall, expected benefits from IOS are always targeted for customer side, regardless of level in the supply chain where IOS is implemented. Win-win situation is considered to be achieved from long term benefits that accumulate from customer binding. Customer side and the end customer in the end always get the benefits, but in the long term each partner's position will become stronger through competitiveness of the whole supply network.

4 General Planning Characteristics

In all case companies IT-governance issues were decided on the corporate level; general rules for IT planning processes, decision criteria, used methods, and perhaps guidelines for used technologies, standards, and platforms. IT-governance was corporate wide and was considered strategic from nature and belonging to the top management agenda. The responsibility for actual applications was distributed to the business level, planning and deciding on what and when - and paying for applications. Thus, planning for IOS was considered to be rather practical than strategic from nature, new information systems were planned in terms of business needs and only if they enhance the operations directly. Other reasons, such as indirect customer value, were considered much more challenging to justify and get through the decision process.

According to the interviewees, IOSs were generally considered beneficial from business operations' point-of-view. Interviewed companies had very different kinds of IOSs with different kinds of companies, e.g. with suppliers, customers, logistics companies, harbors, and banks, among others. The focus of IOSs was mainly in cost reduction.

Allocation of cost was one of the still open issues without a clear policy. GMM and GBM used a case-by-case decisions policy in cost allocation. GFIC, on the other hand, had an overall policy that every participant covers their own costs and the benefits always go to upstream. Belief behind was that benefit of the customer will eventually be also benefit of the whole business network supplying that customer.

Also, the approaches to planning varied. Based on three organizational modes: markets, hierarchies and networks [17], three planning approaches were identified from literature: 1) hierarchy based on authority and use of power to coordinate, 2) community based on trust and willingness to cooperate, and 3) market based on price mechanism and legally bounding contracts [18], [19]. From these, GBM mostly uses hierarchical approach to IOS planning. Most of the IOS projects are based on existing relationships and what they called 'established mutual understanding of the operations'. Usual IOS development was seen as a quite straightforward process and based on production requirements. On he other hand, GFIC and GMM considered planning to be mainly community-based and GFIC even considered it belonging exclusively to long trusting relationships.

> 'Operational excellence is the most important subject in supplier cooperation and sometimes that means stepping on suppliers' toes to get own harmonization working. In this kind of situation it means controlling the planning process, forcing and covering the costs. However, a win-win situation and sharing the costs is always the target, and a strategic goal is partnership.'
> (GBM director)

The focus of IOS was considered to concentrate too much on simple information transfer and not enough on content issues. Also, initiatives was considered to be too product focused while management of inter-organizational processes limped. The IOS partners' readiness and capabilities were considered diverse. Smaller local suppliers might have difficulties to receive electronic information where as ten times larger MNCs dictate the IOS conditions. This was taken pragmatically in interviewed companies; there is no sense to make immense amount of exceptions to large and complex systems, the one who is more flexible does the changes.

> *'Development is still too product oriented, the process thinking lacks behind. There is no such a thing as one-to-one relationship. Everything that comes also goes somewhere. What is preceding and what is proceeding.'*
> (GBM director)

All companies found it very difficult to measure the benefits of IT investments. For that part, practice seems to be in the same situation as 20 years earlier when it was found that only 10% of organizations conducting Strategic ISP at least attempted to assess the benefits [20]. Benefits were considered to be more often than not indirect. In a time of increasing volumes and business growth it was easy to justify IT-initiatives with efficiency gains, speed, accuracy of decision making and especially with ability to cope with the increasing volumes. But proving that the measured effects resulted from some IT-initiative is difficult as there are so many other factors influencing the same results in a turbulent business environment. In inter-organizational environment the evaluation is even more challenging since work, costs and benefits are distributed unevenly to different partners.

> *'Follow-up evaluation is conducted after a year but it doesn't really consist of measurement, which is difficult. How much influence have markets had and how much the project?'* (GMM manager)
> *'Evaluation of benefits is largely absent in planning process. It might be individually agreed about later evaluation if, for example, there exists a need for further development.'* (GFIC manager)

A general observation was that PIOS is conducted with tools developed for internal planning and external and internal IT application proposals are evaluated according to same criteria. A popular MIS topic of Business-IT alignment was evaluated to be high in case companies; business units owned and were responsible for business applications. Also, attitude toward IOS partners and the planning approach depends on overall partner strategy and existing business plans for network development. IT department was not considered to be the initiator of IOSs.

Case companies had a clear, experience based insight that use of a systematic planning method is beneficial for success. Also, it was considered that current planning methods don't consider inter-organizational planning sufficiently. It was perceived that planning in inter-organizational environment differs from internal planning. Thus, need for systematic methods and planning guidelines for PIOS were obvious. Tentative critical success factors for PIOS are presented in next section as identified by interviewed companies.

5 Critical Success Factors for PIOS

During the interviews the company representatives were asked to tell what they considered being the most important success factors for successful PIOS. Following 10 factors were spontaneously expressed:

- GMM interviewees highlighted the importance of the following success factors in IOS planning:
    1. Mutual understanding what will be done
    2. Mutual understanding what benefits are being sought.
    3. Realistic understanding on needed resources. (Bigger partners usually know really well their own resources and capabilities but smaller companies don't seem to. Emergence of IT service providers, integrators, who convey and convert messages, has made system linkages with smaller partners easier.)
- GBM interviewees highlighted the importance of the following success factors in IOS planning:
    1. IT competences and resources; GBM knows really well their own IT competences but sometimes supplier's response 'can be done' is not so assuring. If there is an operator who already knows supplier's systems it's easier to get on discussion on right issues to make sufficiently rigorous specification for operator to implement. Identification and availability of these resources with right competences is the most important factor.
    2. Feasibility; if there is a win-win situation and initiative is in accordance of both parties' strategies it is easy to get resources. If only one sided benefits, then negotiation on price effects, a good feasibility study and a technical specification is needed.
    3. Means menu; decision on development approach, one project at the time or one B2B relationship at the time. E.g. if some supplier has many different systems needed in cooperation, development requires gradual / project at the time style of development. The maturity of suppliers IT systems largely defines the approach.
    4. Planning process; Right people from right organizational levels are needed to do right things. It is as simple as that.
    5. Cultural issues; GBM is operating in global environment and customary IT planning process will affect users spread out globally. Different cultural issues and language barriers makes the planning process more challenging.
- GFIC interviewees highlighted the importance of the following success factors in IOS planning:
    1. Business case; no IT-project will be started without payback. Even if there is a new interesting technology like RFID, it won't be implemented without clear business case. Yet, the payback can be indirect and in the long-term, as in many joint projects with customers.

2. Mutual objectives; there have to be mutual benefits from the project and mutually agreed target. Forcing (hierarchical approach) just won't work and contractual development might stop when the contract's minimum requirements are fulfilled, which is usually inadequate in the long term. Trusting relationship and mutual agreement is needed.

After the interviews all 10 expressed factors from different companies were collected together, analyzed for common and unique emphasis, and abstracted to 7 factors contributing for success. Some of the factors that companies were spontaneously able to articulate were partly or totally overlapping, some factors included multiple issues according to the analysis. However, since the resulting 7 factors were formulated by the researcher, though based on interview material, this collection of factors required further verification from case companies.

The 7 factors and how they were derived were:

1. Target; mutual understanding of what benefits are sought. Interviewees highlighted that all participants should receive benefits (win-win situation). Otherwise further negotiations are needed (e.g. on price effect) to get benefits for everyone. This factor was derived from GMM factor 2, GBM factor 2 and GFIC factor 2 and was straightforwardly derived from original factors.

2. Resource requirements; realistic understanding what IT competencies and resources are needed for realize benefits. Interviewees highlighted that sometimes suppliers might be too optimistic on their IT competences and resource requirements. This factor was straightforwardly derived from GMM factor 3 and GBM factor 1.

3. Payback; direct or indirect benefits will have to overweight needed resources. This factor was a little tricky, since in a way it is a combination of the previous two factors. The two previous factors highlight the perspective that participants understand the target and resource requirements (mutual understanding). This third factor, on the other hand, highlights the fact that IT projects are investments that has to have a payback. This factor was derived from GFIC factor 1 and partly from GBM factor 2 (feasibility study).

4. Planning process; right people from right organizational levels are needed to do right things. This factor highlights the practical experience of interviewees that use of systematic planning approach is beneficial for success. This factor was derived from GBM factor 4 and supported by all case discussion.

5. Trusting relationship; inter-organizational planning need to be based upon mutual trust. This factor was included in GFIC factor 2 but is different from understanding or having mutual objectives. Both GFIC and GMM highlighted this factor for planning, and even GBM considered IOS-planning being based only on established relationships.

6. Means menu; mutual understanding what will be done and how. Derived from GMM factor 1 and GBM factor 3 this factor identifies how and in how many steps the target should be reached. If the maturity of supplier is not very high, a one-step development project might not be possible.

7. Cultural issues; considering and overcoming different cultures of whatever organizational, national or ethnic. Derived from GBM factor 5 this factor might affect to success of planning in multi-national and inter-organizational context.

Company representatives were sent this list of abstracted 7 factors and asked to give a rough weight with a very simple evaluation scale: 1) not at all important, 2) somewhat important, and 3) critical for success. Objective was to be able to create a robust and a tentative model of the most important critical success factors for further research. As these factors were spontaneously proposed by the companies themselves it was expected that companies wouldn't evaluate any of the factors (at least their own) as non-important. Rather, the purpose of this evaluation was to find out companies' collective perspective on what are the most critical success factors.

Table 2. Company specific evaluation on critical success factors (1= not at all important, 2=somewhat important, 3= critical for success)

Factor / Company	GMM	GBM	GFIC	Average
1. Target	3	3	3	3,00
2. Resource requirements	2	3	2	2,33
3. Payback	3	3	3	3,00
4. Planning process	3	3	2	2,67
5. Trusting relationship	3	2	2	2,33
6. Means menu	3	3	3	3,00
7. Cultural issues	3	2	2	2,33

As a result of this second evaluation of the critical success factors for PIOS, a 3-tier model was formulated (picture 1). In the picture the first tier include only factors that all companies considered critical for success (3x3 evaluations). Second tier includes factors that at least two of the companies considered critical (2x3 and 1x2 evaluations) and the third tier includes those factors that were considered critical by at least one company (1x3 and 2x2 evaluations). Company specific evaluations of different factors are described in Table 2.

The resulting three CSFs in the tier 1 form the core of PIOS. However, neither they nor the tier 2 factor of planning process are strictly characteristics for inter-organizational context. Rather, all these four factors could be considered critical for internal planning context as well. Any project will definitely benefit if the target is clear and valuable and a way to reach it is known. Also, the use of a systematic planning process was found to secure better results. Only the content of these factors is more complicated in IOS context.

Understanding the needed resources in the planning process was not considered critical as long as the business benefits will eventually exceed them (the payback). Interestingly, trusting relationships was eventually not considered extremely critical for success. Companies did highlight that planning with partners from different countries and cultural origins affect the planning process, but the cultural issues are something that these global manufacturing companies have to deal with everyday life and, thus, it is not critical factor especially for PIOS.

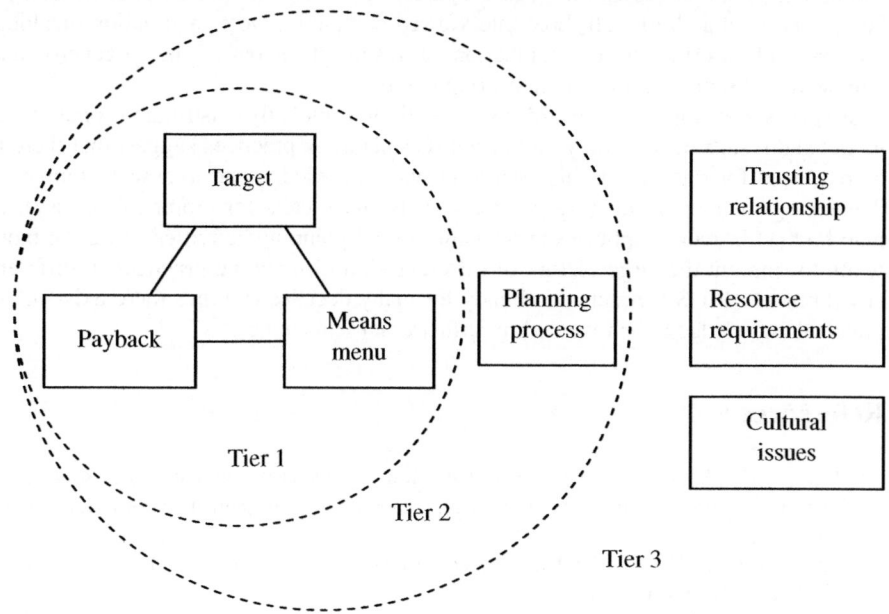

Fig. 1. Three-tier model of critical success factors for PIOS

6 Conclusions

This study among large global manufacturers show that although IOSs are being built somewhat three decades already the planning process for IOS has not received enough attention. All three companies considered that with a systematic planning process the IT implementation process is much more successful or at least the process is more reliable to provide successful outcome. All three companies also considered that planning of inter-organizational information systems is much more complicated than within the company and bears some distinct planning features which are not well covered in current IT-planning guidelines. Yet, the most critical factors for success in planning of IOSs that companies emphasized are quite common for all kind of development projects. It seems that, regardless of planning context for information systems, the most critical factors for success remains similar and only the content of these factors get different emphasis. For example, understanding the target and benefits sought as well as needed resources are needed in any kind of project, but gets more complicated in PIOS since costs and benefits might be unevenly distributed for different participants. Thus, a win-win situation and development of overall competitiveness was highlighted.

This issue of inter-organizational planning for joint information systems has become increasingly relevant among companies since extensive development in organizations to concentrate only to core competencies and processes, and to strategically outsource other processes where appropriate. High dependency on business network increases the need for careful planning and close cooperation with key partners. In addition, all three interviewed companies were in situation of global process and information harmonization, a result of increased heterogeneity and complexity of rapid organic and non-organic growth.

Business development toward networked and globally distributed operational model and results of this study on current IOS planning practices suggest that there is a great need for research in this area to provide knowledge and to assists companies developing their own planning practices. This study calls for empirical research to map both 1) in more depth of inter-organizational planning activities and 2) in more width to find out the large picture of different kind of planning practices in different environments. PIOS is practiced already for many decades and thus there exists large practical knowledge to be revealed in further empirical studies.

References

1. Dyer, J.H., Singh, H.: The relational view: cooperative strategy and sources of interorganizational competitive advantage. Academy of Management Review 23(4), 660–679 (1998)
2. Prahalad, C.K., Hamel, G.: The core competence of the corporation. Harvard Business Review 68(3), 79–91 (1990)
3. Quinn, J.B., Hilmer, F.G.: Strategic Outsourcing. MIT Sloan Management Review 35(4), 43–55 (1994)
4. Dickson, G.W., Leitheiser, R.L., Nechis, M., Wetherbe, J.C.: Key Information System Issues for the 1980's. MIS Quarterly 8(3), 135–148 (1984)
5. Boynton, A.C., Zmud, R.W.: Information Technology Planning in the 1990's: Directions for Practice and Research. MIS Quarterly 11(1), 58–71 (1987)
6. Li, E.Y., Chen, H.-G.: Output-driven information system planning: a case study. Information & Management 38(3), 185–199 (2001)
7. Humphreys, P.K., Lai, M.K., Sculli, D.: An inter-organizational information system for supply chain management. International Journal of Production Economics 70(3), 245–255 (2001)
8. Webster, J.: Networks of collaboration or conflict? Electronic data interchange and power in the supply chain. The Journal of Strategic Information Systems 4(1), 31–42 (1995)
9. Segev, A., Porra, J., Roldan, M.: Internet-based EDI strategy. Decision Support Systems 21(3), 157–170 (1997)
10. Driedonks, C., Gregor, S., Wassenaar, A., Van Heck, E.: Economic and Social Analysis of the Adoption of B2B Electronic Marketplaces: A Case Study in the Australian Beef Industry. International Journal of Electronic Commerce 9(3), 49–72 (2005)
11. Robey, D., Im, G., Wareham, J.D.: Theoretical Foundations of Empirical Research on Interorganizational Systems: Assessing Past Contributions and Guiding Future Directions. Journal of the Association for Information Systems 9, 497–518 (2008)
12. Eisenhardt, K.M., Graebner, M.E.: Theory building from cases: opportunities and challenges. Academy of Management Journal 50, 25–32 (2007)
13. Cunningham, J.B.: Case study principles for different types of cases. Quality & Quantity 31, 401–423 (1997)

14. Sarker, S., Lee, S.: Using a Case Study to Test the Role of Three Key Social Enablers in ERP Implementation. In: Proceedings of the Twenty First International Conference on Information Systems, pp. 414–425. Association of Information Systems, Atlanta (2000)
15. Akkermans, H., Van Helden, K.: Vicious and virtuous cycles in ERP implementation: a case study of interrelations between critical success factors. European Journal of Information Systems 11(1), 35–46 (2002)
16. Rajagopal, P.: An innovation-diffusion view of implementation of enterprise resource planning (ERP) systems and development of a research model. Information & Management 40(2), 87–114 (2002)
17. Thorelli, H.B.: Networks: Between markets and hierarchies. Strategic Management Journal 7(1), 37–51 (1986)
18. Ciborra, C.: Research agenda for transaction costs approach to information systems. In: Boland, R., Hirschheim, R. (eds.) Critical Issues in Information Systems Research, pp. 253–274. Wiley, New York (1987)
19. Adler, P.S.: Market, Hierarchy and Trust: The Knowledge Economy and the Future of Capitalism. Organisation Science 12(2), 215–235 (2001)
20. Galliers, R.D.: Information systems planning in the United Kingdom and Australia - a comparison of current practice. Oxford Surveys in Information Technology 4, 223–255 (1987)

Exploring the Characteristics of Information Systems Maintenance – Defining Focus and Content through Objects

Malin Nordström, Karin Axelsson, and Ulf Melin

Linköping University, Department of Management and Engineering,
SE-581 83 Linköping, Sweden
{malin.nordstrom,karin.axelsson,ulf.melin}@liu.se

Abstract. The purpose of this paper is to explore the characteristics of information systems (IS) maintenance within an IT and organizational setting. We discuss the characteristics of maintenance objects' focus and content. Our results are based on qualitative case studies. In this paper a case study of a Swedish Bank is used to illustrate our discussion. Our findings show that maintenance objects can be defined by processes and/or functions or products and/or services within an organizational setting. This is done in order to increase a business perspective in maintenance management and to clarify roles of responsibility for organizational changes required from new IT capabilities. According to our findings maintenance objects can contain business solutions and IT solutions. This implies that business beneficial maintenance is supported by close cooperation between actors from the organizational setting and the IT organization. The result of the paper is a characterization of IS maintenance through definition of maintenance objects' focus and content.

Keywords: IS maintenance, IS maintenance management, Maintenance objects, Information systems.

1 Introduction

Increasing demands from customers or other clients regarding, for example, cost reductions, high quality and value for money (ROI), imply among other things that information systems (IS) maintenance organizations need to be more effective. Higher functionality and stability in the IT solution portfolio, and overall quality in core business, and at the same time lower IS maintenance costs is an equation that is often difficult to solve. To meet the increasing demands, maintenance organizations have to deal with the ability to further develop and maintain IS. This is not an easy task and requires an adequate management system, which has to satisfy a number of not always homogenous needs [1]. Some twenty years ago, Colter [9] stated that the greatest problem of software maintenance is of managerial nature rather than technical. Sneed and Brössler [28] developed this argument further by identifying success factors for software maintenance, and they mean that success in maintenance can not only be measured by cost reduction and user satisfaction – this is an over-simplification of a far more complex issue (ibid.).

H. Salmela and A. Sell (Eds.): SCIS 2011, LNBIP 86, pp. 112–123, 2011.
© Springer-Verlag Berlin Heidelberg 2011

Definitions of system maintenance often stress the post-delivery characteristics and define system maintenance to be different types of changes [16]. In these definitions management is seen as part of the change activities. This kind of categorizations of changes originates from Lientz' and Swanson's dissertation in 1980 [19], but has been further developed by many researchers and practitioners since then [7]. Measurements indicate that most of the change activities aim to improve and adapt IS to changed environments. Researchers therefore mean that "maintenance" is too narrow as a concept and prefer the concept "evolution" (ibid). Their point is that maintenance is associated with corrective activities, rather than further development. Another dimension of the definition of maintenance is that the concept has been criticized as being too narrow because of its delimited substance of change activities. Researchers also seem to agree that system maintenance is quite unfairly treated and therefore underexplored, in theory and practice, in relation to its importance for organizations (ibid).

The most recommended means of control for maintenance is management by actions or management by contracts. The most common way to control this is maintenance process management and service level agreements (SLA). SLA's often contain agreements concerning availability, opening hours and response time. The lack of common processes for specific maintenance activities is often pointed out as an explanation to ad-hoc maintenance management [1]. Another common means of control is management by objectives, but we have not found much literature about managing maintenance by business objectives. We actually find this quite strange, because in a maintenance situation there is an opportunity to measure the benefit of IT investments, benefits that are often more or less well defined in business cases that have preceded IT investments. A possible explanation for this is that maintenance often is performed from an IT perspective (a more narrow technology focus) which puts the business perspective in the background. This kind of more isolated IS maintenance does not normally admit management by business objectives because the business objectives are not known by the maintainers. The two roles that are outlined in literature representing businesses are user and customer [1; 17], but none of these roles are members of a maintenance organization. Instead, they are expected to formulate their needs in a request for change or equivalent (ibid).

IT focused maintenance, based on a technological focus, as described above, can over time mean that the IS no longer supports the current organizational needs because the relations between IT maintenance organizations and customers and users are not clarified [22]. Time is an important factor for this situation. Organizational settings change over time and it is also common that IS are used for new business processes different from the original purpose (ibid). Thus, in this paper we argue that the business perspective in maintenance management must become more explicit.

The maintenance management challenge is well known by both researchers and practitioners, but practitioners are still – in many settings – struggling with the management problem. Since there are other resources that are maintained as well, such as buildings and stock portfolios, it is reasonable to assume that the characteristics of the maintenance object are important for management. The purpose of this paper is to explore the characteristics of IS maintenance within an IT and organizational setting. We discuss the characteristics of maintenance objects' focus and content. Our idea is to use the maintenance object to organize maintenance management and thereby clarify maintenance assignments. The research questions in the present paper are; (1) how can maintenance objects be focused and (2) what will the objects contain?

The paper is organized as follows. After this introduction we identify some important theoretical points of departure for the study in section 2, and in section 3 the research design is presented. Section 4 describes the case study at a Swedish Bank. In section 5 we analyze our empirical data. Finally, in section 6 our conclusions and ideas for further research are presented.

2   Theoretical Points of Departure

In this section we describe and discuss some theoretical statements that we used as theoretical points of departure when we carried out the case study presented below.

2.1   IT Systems Creating Benefits within Organizations

In the IS field the concept "information system" originally was defined as encompassing both computerized information processing and manual information processing [8; 13; 18]. Thus, theoretically the IS concept is wider than computerized information processing (e.g. as typically defined in the computer science discipline [cf. 29]), but in practice IS is often interpreted as a system for computerized information processing. To clarify the distinction between what is computerized or not we choose to use other concepts; IT system is used for the computerized information processing and organizational setting for activities that are performed with or without the aid of IT systems. We also use the terms process and function for subsets in an organizational setting.

Niessink and van Vliet [21] introduce a service perspective on maintenance and argue for a difference between development and maintenance in the light of products and services. They mean that while the result of a development activity is a product, the result of a maintenance activity is a service. But at the same time they mention that the differences between products and services are not clear in the marketing literature (ibid.). The starting point for their argument is the IT organization which has to fulfill the needs of software for current businesses in order to create business value and benefits of IT.

Statements concerning IT systems and organizational settings also influence the content of maintenance objects. There is a difference between maintaining the IT system or maintaining the IT system *and* the organizational setting. Several authors argue for the intertwined nature of IS in action and organizational settings [e.g., 23; 24; 29], sometimes with inspiration from symbolic interactions [6]. Maintaining the IT system and the organizational setting is obviously not reasonable as an assignment for a maintenance organization, as it would mean that the maintenance organization is responsible for the organizational setting. However, establishing the boundary is not as easy as it seems because at the same time as the maintenance organization maintains an IT system it also maintains a computerized organizational setting – embedded in the IT system. This implies that IT systems are an intertwined part of organizational settings and have socio-material dimensions [23; 24; 29]. This also implies that IT systems are supporting actions in organizational settings [8; 15; 32]. With an increasing use of IT systems, more and more in the organizational setting is maintained by maintenance organizations. This situation may lead to unclear roles of responsibility between maintenance organizations and organizations or parts of organizations that perform the current business tasks in the organization.

In the IS field, it is also common to initially perform a business analysis before development or change of IT systems [2]. This also goes for other change attempts such as Total Quality Management (TQM) [12]. In TQM evaluations of business processes are a part of an ongoing process of continuous improvement. In software maintenance theory there is no such evident tradition, which may partly be explained by the development of system maintenance theory in the Software Engineering area where the IS is seen as a product rather than an integrated part of the business, in line with the perspective outline above. An early study that stressed the importance of a business perspective was Bendifallah and Scacchi [4]. They conducted a study of IT system maintenance from a user perspective and thereby studied the organizational setting and how it interacts with the IT systems. Their conclusion was that in order to understand the system maintenance, one must understand the surrounding organizational setting and the users' and the maintainers' situation (ibid). More recent studies have stressed the maintenance practice [27; 28], but only a few have emphasized the importance of a clarified business perspective. The organizational setting that the IT system supports is, thus, implicit in much research.

A maintenance organization without a maintenance object is quite meaningless, but in software maintenance research the object's focus and content are treated rather unreflecting and are not investigated thoroughly. Concepts such as software, systems or products are used frequently but are not analyzed any further. Kitchenham et al. [17 p. 370] talk, e.g., about the maintained object in terms of *"the software application, product or package that is undergoing modification. A product is a conglomerate of a number of different artifacts"*. Further, they discuss how the product is influenced by domains, age, maturity composition, and quality (ibid.).

2.2 Organizing Maintenance Settings

As mentioned above, an organizational setting perspective highlights what is done, with or without IT systems, and the need to focus IT as an integrated part of an organization. IT systems are related to activities performed in the organizational setting rather than to the organization per se. Maintenance is complex with many internal and external parties involved, which makes it necessary to distinguish between activities performed in the organizational setting and the organization. Otherwise there is a risk that maintenance still lacks influence from a business perspective. In order to analyze system maintenance we have redefined the concept through different sub categories. The two main concepts are organizational setting and IT setting, which is a consequence of our intention to increase the business perspective in maintenance management theory. Organizational setting is a generic concept and includes any kind of activities, thus, system maintenance is conducted in all kinds of organizations that use IT systems. By IT setting we mean the technically oriented work that is carried out to handle IT systems. Based on the understanding of IT as a natural and intertwined part of an organizational setting [23; 24; 29] we also view systems maintenance as including organizational processes and/or functions and IT. We illustrate maintenance as a subset of both the organizational setting and the IT setting (figure 1).

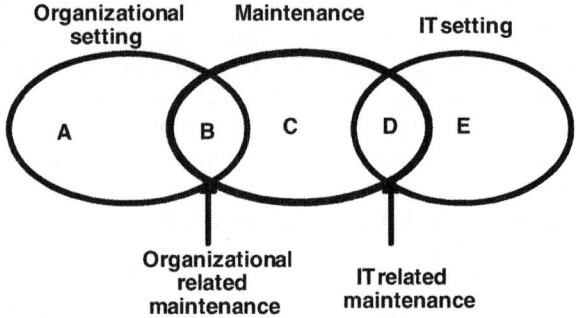

Fig. 1. Maintenance as a subset of the organizational setting and the IT setting

The perspective of maintenance as a subset of the organizational setting and the IT setting results in two sub-categories of maintenance; organizational related maintenance (field B in figure 1) and IT related maintenance (field D in figure 1). Field C is formed by a common management of field B and D that arises since maintenance is a subset of the organizational setting and the IT setting. The activity is of a managing character (i.e., giving and taking assignments).

Nordström and Welander [22] argue for a high influence from the current organizational setting in a maintenance organization in order to increase the benefit of IT systems over time.

3 Research Design

The results presented in this paper originate from a research project with a wider scope containing three case studies (a Swedish Bank, a Telecom Company and a Swedish Authority). In this paper we explore the focus and content of maintenance objects within the Swedish Bank's domestic and international payments. The studied maintenance objects have, in the research project, been used as means to organize maintenance activities. The research project has been performed with a pragmatic perspective. We agree with Wicks and Freeman [31] as well as Cronen [10] that a pragmatic view allows the researcher to see the value of theories as an aid to predict phenomenon, and also manages people's actions in order to improve organizational settings. Within a pragmatic approach, practical use of research findings is highly valued, and therefore we have chosen a qualitative interpreting research approach. Interpretive research, within the IS discipline, concentrates on creating an understanding for the IT system in context [e.g., 29]. The researchers are therefore interested in how IT systems are influenced by the context, and how IT systems influence the organizational setting [20; 30]. Qualitative case studies have been used in the present research project combined with an action research (AR) approach. AR is often used in the IS discipline [3]. The purpose of AR is to improve the studied object at the same time as scientific knowledge is developed (ibid.). The empirical data has been analyzed following a qualitative, interpreting approach [30].

The case study at the Swedish Bank contained three phases; object inventory, object modeling, and proposal for organizing the maintenance practice. Phase 1 and 2 are focused in this paper. Phase 1 – the object inventory – started with a definition of the organizational setting to make it understandable to the researchers. The information was collected by interviews with 20 key persons. The key persons had roles of responsibility for payment products, market segments, sales channels, payment processes or IT systems. The interviews were documented and resulted in lists of payment products, market segments, sales channel, payment processes, and IT systems and their relations. In this phase we discussed the maintenance objects during a workshop with key actors from the Bank. In the last phase we made a proposal for organizing maintenance according to Nordström and Welander [22].

4 Payments at the Bank – Findings from a Case Study

The researchers got the AR assignment to reorganize maintenance practice at the Bank in order to use the IT systems in a more effective way. The maintenance practice was fragmented with highly delegated responsibilities, which led to a lack of a holistic view and ineffective use of resources. The maintenance practice was also characterized by a high level of key person dependence. Producers of the payments were the Department of Private and Commercial Payments with approximately 150 employees. The payment practice was divided into four subsets:

- Payment production
- Product development and maintenance
- IT development, maintenance and production
- Marketing

The range of products consisted of approximately 40 payment products, for example corporate payments, private payment and bank-to-bank payments. The main clients were Bank clients via their own bank. The products were accessible via sales channels such as the phone, web, ATM, and bank office. There were also approximately 40 IT systems which primarily supported the payment process. The maintenance was organized with the help of seven maintenance objects in which IT systems were grouped together. The underlying ground for the grouping of IT systems showed signs of:

- Organizational boundaries
- Design of IT systems
- Personnel extent
- Dependence of key persons

With the result from the object inventory the IT systems were analyzed from the view of process, products, sales channels, and market segments. Together with key persons from the payment department we then discussed the consequences of the different object grounds. During the test we found out that a combination of a product and/or service and process and/or function view was the most effective way to group IT systems in order to create clarified maintenance assignments. The organizational grouping was rejected because of constant reorganizing of the line organization, and because the complexity of internal and external parties. The IT system design grouping was rejected because of its volume and because of the lack of business perspective. When we used the process and/or function or product and/or service perspective we found out that we avoided the above mentioned problems. But because of the IT systems multi-functional nature we sometimes had IT systems that supported several processes and/or functions. However, no attempt to share IT systems between objects was done. We used the dominance principle and in borderline cases the IT system was placed into the object in which organizational setting it was primarily used. Together with the participants from the Bank we formed three maintenance objects; Payments, Warehouse, and Clearing.

The first, and most extensive, was Payments. In that object we brought together every payment IT system regardless of whether they supported domestic or international payment products, and independent of which market segment the payment product belonged to. This was done as a difference to the existing maintenance objects in which domestic and international payments and market segments were separated. The object Warehouse contained IT systems supporting complementary products to payments, such as autogiro and BankID. The object Clearing was performed independently of the current product and therefore we chose to put it in a separate object. The participants from the Bank thought that this new object structure, with new bounds of responsibility, gave them the opportunity to;

- Clarify maintenance assignments
- Eliminate competition between products and IT systems
- Decommission non-profitable products and their IT systems
- Merge domestic and international payment products
- Differentiate between products and IT systems
- Use IT systems and employees in a more effective way

With the wider scope and with a clarified business perspective, it became obvious for the maintainers at the Bank that they are maintaining something more than only a technical IT system. Only a few matters of their daily work concern the IT systems from a technical point of view. Together with the participants we started to talk about Business Solutions as the organizational setting view of an IT system and IT Solution as the technical view of an IT system. We found out that a Business Solution may contain IT functions, documents and added value from the maintenance organization. We created for example a Business Solution for Knowledge Support containing computerized help instructions together with paper based guidelines. The added value from the maintenance organization was to adapt them to the target group. The findings of Business Solutions as a part of the maintenance object gave the Bank the opportunity to clarify roles of responsibility for the organizational setting perspective of the IT system. Later they also pointed out roles of responsibility and documented clarified maintenance assignments with the maintenance object as a starting point.

5 Characteristics of IS Maintenance

In this section we relate our empirical findings from the Bank study to our theoretical statements presented earlier in the paper.

5.1 Maintenance Objects' Focus

Our first research question was related to the focus of maintenance objects. The case study at the Bank showed us the possibility of focusing maintenance objects within a products and/or services or process and/or function view. Together with the action perspective on IT systems [14; 15; 32], which states that IT systems perform actions in organizational settings, and the results from the case study, our conclusion is that maintenance objects should be focused by products and/or services (Payments and Warehouse at the Bank) or process and/or functions (Clearing at the Bank). Organizational boundaries were rejected as a focus definer because of constant re-organization in the line organization. From a theoretical view organization is not a good focus definer either, because IT systems have relations to actions performed in the organizational setting rather than to the organization itself. However, in a situation where IT systems are used by different internal and even external parties it is necessary to clarify the difference between actions in the organizational setting and the organization. Otherwise it is possible that maintenance organizations are only manned from an organizational view and the maintenance still lacks business perspectives and objectives.

In the case study at the Bank we had no discussions about the extent of the maintenance objects or sharing of IT systems between maintenance objects because of their multi-functionality from an organizational setting view. However, this could be an issue in situations with large maintenance objects, but maybe foremost from a theoretical view. Even our most extended maintenance object at the Bank – Payments – did not trigger any extent discussions. In the Bank study there were no problems with IT systems that supported several products and/or services. However, the extent of maintenance objects and also multi-functional IT systems are factors to take into consideration when defining the focus of maintenance objects.

To summarize, we suggest four factors to take into consideration when defining the focus of maintenance objects;

- Work practice products and services
- Product independent processes
- The extent of the maintenance objects
- Multi-functional IT systems

5.2 Maintenance Objects' Content

Our second research question concerned the content of maintenance objects. Our results are based on the action perspective of IS, where IT systems have an organizational dimension as well as a technical one (as stated above). In the case study at the Bank we started to name the organizational setting dimension "Business Solution" and the technical dimension "IT Solution". In order to increase the organizational setting dimension and to clarify business objectives and roles of responsibility, our conclusion therefore is that a maintenance object should contain Business Solutions and IT Solutions. Together they are used in an organizational setting to produce products and/or services. In figure 2 below, we have further developed figure 1 by adding Business Solutions and IT Solutions.

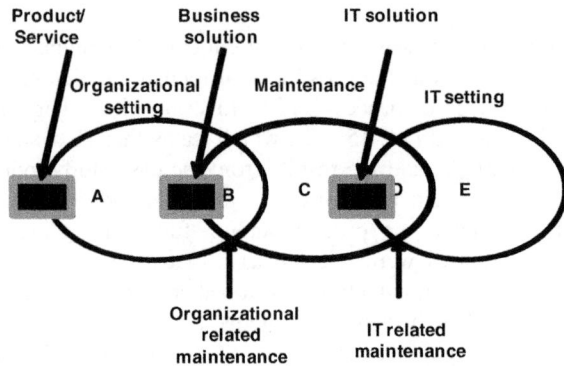

Fig. 2. Maintenance objects' content

This resulted in the following discussion: An IT solution is the maintenance object for IT related maintenance (field D) which is performed by internal or external IT suppliers. The IT Solution is also the delivery of the IT related maintenance to the organizational related maintenance (field B). Organizational related maintenance is performed by parties who are involved in current actions in the organizational setting. At the Bank it was persons working with or responsible for payments. Organizational setting maintenance has Business Solutions as their maintenance objects which also are their delivery to parties who perform current actions in the organizational setting (field A). This means that we adopt a service perspective on maintenance. In line with Niessink and van Vliet [21] we want to use the service perspective to create clarified maintenance assignments, but with this statement we go beyond their conclusion, as we combine a service and a product perspective.

With a wider scope of maintenance objects it was also possible for the maintainers at the Bank to take the responsibility for described business processes (payments) and not only for computerized functions. This observation was the starting point for defining Business Solutions as a part of the maintenance objects. A maintenance organization may have the responsibility for computerized work but also for the organizational setting. However, is it not reasonable to take responsibility for the current organizational setting itself? In the case study at the Bank we showed that this is possible with an action perspective on IT systems [14; 15; 32].

IT Solutions contain one or more IT systems or other technical components. Based on the results from the case study at the Bank our conclusion is that Business Solutions contain the following components;

- IT system functions and/or processes
- Described processes and/or functions
- Added value from the maintenance organization

6 Conclusions

In this paper we have analyzed and discussed focus and content of maintenance objects containing IT systems. Field observations related to the consequences of isolated IT system maintenance were the background to the research project. We investigated approaches to increase the business perspective in maintenance work as a way of tackling the management problem in maintenance. Our two research questions concerned focus and content of maintenance objects, which can be used as a starting point to create clarified assignments for maintenance.

Our first conclusion is that maintenance objects could be focused by products and/or services or processes and/or functions in order to increase the business perspective in maintenance. Multi-functional IT systems and the extent of maintenance objects must also be taken into consideration when defining focus for maintenance objects. Our second conclusion is that maintenance objects could contain business solutions and IT solutions to take the organizational setting perspective and the IT system perspective simultaneously into consideration. This means that a business solution can contain a business process with its IT functionality. A business solution also gives the opportunity to clarify roles of responsibility for changes in the organizational setting required by new IT capabilities. The conclusions of the content and focus of maintenance objects lead us to a view where we think it is fruitful to stop talking about maintenance as a technical phenomenon only, and include the organizational setting dimension. These findings are in line with, e.g., Sillito and Wynn [27] whose understanding is that maintenance work is highly context dependent. The complement of maintenance objects containing Business Solutions as well as IT Solutions also means that it is necessary for representatives from the organizational setting to be a part of the maintenance organization. It is not enough to categorize them as customers or users; they must be more thoroughly involved. We argue that it is necessary that persons from the current organizational setting must be permanent members of maintenance organizations in order to improve or guarantee the organizational setting perspective over time.

The results presented in this paper should not be seen as final – rather explorative and emerging results that need to be further validated, investigated and developed in line with a cumulative research tradition. As mentioned above, our conclusions are based on three case studies – one of the cases focused and illustrated in this paper. The results from the studies are similar – a clear pattern appears. We have therefore only presented the case study at the Bank in this paper, but we still need to add more empirical data. However, we find the results interesting enough to be developed further and the case studies have strengthened our idea of the need for an increasing business influence in maintenance activities. To further develop the findings concerning maintenance objects we plan to investigate the relations between maintenance objects. We have developed a framework which aims to describe an organization's collected quantity of maintenance objects in a maintenance object architecture (MOA). Our idea is that the MOA can be used to improve IT governance for maintenance, in the same way as Enterprise Architecture is used to improve IT governance for strategic IT decisions [5; 25]. The MOA will give organizations an overview of the total portfolio of maintenance objects. By using our view of IT systems from an organizational setting context we hope that MOA can be a basis from which the gap between business staff and IT staff can be bridged, which is one of the aims of an IT governance framework [cf. 11; 26].

References

1. April, A., Huffman Hayes, J., Abran, A., Dumke, R.: Software Maintenance Maturity Model (SMMmm): the software maintenance process model. Journal of Software Maintenance and Evolution: Research and Practice (17), 197–223 (2005)
2. Avison, D.E., Fitzgerald, G.: Information Systems Development: Methodologies, Techniques and Tools, 3rd edn. McGraw-Hill, London (1998)
3. Baskerville, R., Myers, M.D.: Making IS research relevant to practice – Foreword. MIS Quarterly Special Issue on Action Research in Information Systems 28(3), 329–335 (2004)
4. Bendifallah, S., Scacchi, W.: Understanding software maintenance work. IEEE Transactions on Software Engineering 13(3), 311–323 (1987)
5. Bernard, S.A.: An introduction to enterprise architecture, Bloomington, IN (2005)
6. Blumer, H.: Symbolic Interactionism: Perspective and method. University of California Press, Barkley (1969)
7. Chapin, N., Hale, J.E., Khan, K.M., Ramil, J.F., Tan, W.-G.: Types of software evolution and software maintenance. Journal of Software Maintenance and Evolution: Research and Practice 13(1), 3–30 (2001)
8. Checkland, P., Holwell: Information, Systems and Information Systems – making sense of the field. Wiley & Sons, Chichester (1998)
9. Colter, M.A.: The business of software maintenance. In: Proceedings of the 1st European Workshop of Software Maintenance. Computer Science Department, p. 12. University of Durham, Durham (1987)
10. Cronen, V.: Practical Theory, Practical Art, and the Pragmatic-Systemic Account of Inquiry. Communication Theory 11(1), 14–35 (2001)
11. de Haes, S., van Grembergen, W.: IT Governance and its mechanisms. Information Systems Control Journal 1 (2004)
12. Deming, W.E.: Out of the Crisis. Massachusetts Institute of Technology, Center for Advanced Educational Services, Cambridge, Massachusetts (1982)
13. Galliers, R.: Change as Crisis or Growth? Toward a Trans-disciplinary View of Information Systems as a Field of Study: A Response to Benbasat and Zmud's Call for Returning to the IT Artifact. Journal of the Association for Information Systems 4(6), 337–351 (2003)
14. Goldkuhl, G., Lyytinen, K.: A language action view of information systems. In: Proceeedings of the 3rd International Conference on Information Systems, Ann Arbor, pp. 13–30 (1982)
15. Goldkuhl, G., Ågerfalk, P.J.: IT Artefacts as Socio-Pragmatic Instruments: Reconciling the Pragmatic, Social, Semiotic and Technical. International Journal of Technology and Human Interaction 1(3), 2341–2354 (2005)
16. IEEE, Standard for Software Maintenance, IEEE Std 1219-1998. The Institute of Electrical and Electronics Engineers Inc. (1998)

17. Kitchenham, B.A., Travassos, G.H., von Mayrhauser, A., Niessink, F., Schneidewind, N.F., Singer, J., Takada, S., Vehvilainen, R., Yang, H.: Towards an Ontology of Software Maintenance. Journal of Software Maintenance and Evolution: Research and Practice (11), 365–389 (1999)
18. Langefors, B.: Theoretical Analysis of Information Systems. Studentlitteratur, Lund (1966)
19. Lientz, B., Swanson, E.B.: Software Maintenance Management. Addison-Wesley Publishing, Reading (1980)
20. Myers, M.D., Avison, D.E.: An Introduction to Qualitative Research in Information Systems. In: Myers, M.D., Avison, D.E. (eds.) An Introduction to Qualitative Research in Information Systems, pp. 3–12. Sage Publications Ltd., London (2002)
21. Niessink, F., van Vliet, H.: Software maintenance from a service perspective. Journal of Software Maintenance and Evolution: Research and Practice (12), 103–120 (2000)
22. Nordström, M., Welander, T.: Business Oriented Systems Maintenance Management. In: Khan, K., Zhang, Y. (eds.) Managing Corporate Information Systems Evolution and Maintenance, pp. 326–344. Idea Group Publishing, Hershey (2005)
23. Orlikowski, W.J.: Sociomaterial Practices: Exploring Technology at Work. Organization Studies 28(9), 1435–1448 (2007)
24. Orlikowski, W.J., Scott, S.V.: Sociomateriality: Challenging the Separation of Technology, Work and Organization. The Academy of Managements Annals 2(1), 433–474 (2008)
25. Ross, J.W., Weill, P., Robertson, D.C.: Enterprise Architecture as Strategy. Harvard Business School Press, Boston (2006)
26. Schwertsik, A., Wolf, P., Krcmar, H.: IT-controlling in federal organizations. In: Newell, S., Whitley, E., Pouloudi, N., Wareham, J., Mathiassenl, L. (eds.) Proceeding of the 17th European Conference on Information Systems (ECIS 2009), Verona, Italy, June 8-10, pp. 2158–2169 (2009)
27. Sillito, J., Wynn, E.: The Social Context of Software Maintenance. In: Proceedings of the International Conference of Software Maintenance, pp. 325–334. IEEE Computer Society, Paris (2007)
28. Sneed, H., Brössler, P.: Critical Success Factors in Software Maintenance A Case Study. In: Proceedings of the International Conference on Software Maintenance, p. 190. IEEE Computer Society, Amsterdam (2003)
29. Walsham, G.: Interpreting Information Systems in Organizations. Wiley & Sons, Chichester (1993)
30. Walsham, G.: Doing interpretive research. European Journal of Information Systems 15(3), 320–330 (2006)
31. Wicks, A.C., Freeman, R.E.: Organization Studies and the New Pragmatism: Positivism, Anti-positivism, and the Search for Ethics. Organization Science, Institute for Operations Research and the Management Sciences 9(2), 123–140 (1998)
32. Winograd, T., Flores, F.: Understanding computers and cognition: A new foundation for design. Ablex, Norwood (1986)

Investigating Culture in IT Offshoring: A Literature Review

Tingting Lin

Turku Centre for Computer Science (TUCS)
Turku School of Economics, Turku University,
Joukahaisenkatu 3-5 B, 6th floor, FI-20520 Turku
Tingting.lin@tse.fi

Abstract. IT offshoring has become a prominent subject in IT/IS research, attracting much research attention on its various aspects. The presence of culture in the field of IT offshoring has been increasingly investigated since the millennium, but an overall view is lacking. This article presents a literature review for a comprehensive understanding of culture throughout the lifecycle of IT offshoring. The analysis of 24 articles from pertinent academic outlets shows research trends and gaps in the relevant academic field, and proposes a practical framework for future research. For IT offshoring researchers, the paper provides a summary of prior research on the aspect of culture. The results are also valuable for practitioners to investigate their own IT offshoring relations. Most importantly, the review identifies needs for future research on this topic.

Keywords: Literature review, IT offshoring, culture.

1 Introduction

The pace of globalization has brought a major shift in the software industry – from utilizing internal production to seeking for international partnerships, such as offshoring. Despite the heated debates spurred by this controversial issue, offshoring has become an important milestone in the evolution of global economics [1]. In academia, IT offshoring is not an unacquainted topic. Many researchers have been investigating the offshoring of IT from various aspects. Ravichandran and Ahmed [2] presented a framework which consists of project suitability and site evaluation in the offshoring of information system development. Smith, Mitra and Narasimhan [3] examined the offshoring of software development and maintenance on the basis of resource, environment and project management. Khan and Fitzgerald [4] studied offshoring decision making, advancing four elements of significance: organizational factors, technological factors, geographical/environmental factors, and process factors. Furthermore, Carmel and Tjia [1] brought forward in their book the fundamentals of offshoring with extensive review of its historical context and future landscape, and examination of its most critical business issues and risks.

Most of the identified issues stem from the geographically distributed work across cultures. On one hand, successful offshoring work requires awareness and respect of cultural differences among team members [1]. On the other hand, culture is often

H. Salmela and A. Sell (Eds.): SCIS 2011, LNBIP 86, pp. 124–137, 2011.

blamed, at least partially, in organizational failures [5]. Therefore, the evaluation on the influence of culture, as well as the search for effective cross-cultural management has attracted increasing research attention in the field of IT offshoring. However, an overall view is lacking across all the studies conducted on this subject. To establish a comprehensive understanding of the relationship between culture and IT offshoring, the author believes that a literature review can provide an overview of the existent achievement in the relevant academic field, and hence form a solid foundation leading to future development of new theories and propositions. For these objectives, this literature review endeavours to address the following research questions:

- What are the emerging research themes on culture in IT offshoring?
- What are the most adopted methodologies in the relevant studies?
- How does culture affect IT offshoring activities?
- How can the existent knowledge be advanced in the future research?

The review analyses 24 articles on IT offshoring with a primary focus on culture, through their methodologies, insights and findings. It incorporates different levels of culture with relevant IT offshoring perspectives into a summary of six themes, and identifies research trends and gaps through the literature. In the end, a practical framework is presented for future research, illustrating the immersion of the whole IT offshore lifecycle in the related culture environment.

2   Background

2.1   What Is IT Offshoring?

The concept of IT offshoring has been widely discussed by researchers and practitioners since 1990's. It is characterized by the shifting of activities to lower-cost nations. Jahns, Hartmann and Bals [6] argue that the offshoring concept should be delimited from "offshore outsourcing", thus incorporating external outsourcing, internal job relocation, as well as a hybrid option of joint venture established in offshore locations. Hence, business practices on the offshoring of IT can be categorized in three models: (1) Offshore outsourcing, (2) captive offshoring, and (3) joint venture. Since the third model, namely joint venture, is a hybrid model of the preceding two, cultural implications for this model will be included in the research of offshore outsourcing and captive offshoring. Thus, to simplify the categorization, this research will only focus on the first two models. When the provider of tasks and processes is from a third party which is beyond the boundary of the organization, it can be defined as outsourcing. Offshore outsourcing is the outsourcing activities carried out in a country other than the home country. Involving more cross-border and cross-culture activities, offshore outsourcing would considerably complicate the supply chain. Meanwhile, it also offers unprecedented economic potentials and opportunities. Therefore, offshore outsourcing deserves to be studied much from the purchasing perspective [6]. Nevertheless, the emerging model of captive offshoring cannot be neglected. The strategy of captive offshoring is usually pursued by multinational companies to maintain complete control of their offshore operations, when activities are still conducted within the same organization. Besides the main purpose of the overall cost reduction, the captive model can also enable the organization to leverage learning and knowledge through global best practices across various captive centres to enhance the overall capabilities and flexibility [7].

Besides the concept of IT offshoring, it is also necessary to shortly clarify the scope of IT in this research. The author adapts to Carmel and Tjia's scope of IT in the offshoring context [1]. As they suggested, IT is not segregated from software. All kinds of software-related activities are included: IT service and IT applications, software products, and embedded software. Moreover, the offshoring of IT-enabled services (ITES), e.g. call centres, are also considered due to its tight connection with IT offshoring.

2.2 Culture in the Context of IT Offshoring

The understanding of culture as a term is often a challenge in culture-related studies. Though there is abundant literature to reference, the difficulties are simultaneously generated from the multitude of definitions, frameworks and dimensions available to describe this concept [8]. Thus models are needed to conceptualize culture in a related research as abstraction under the complexity of cultural characteristics. This research adapts to Karahanna, Evaristo and Srite's [9] multi-layer model of culture constructed around values and practices. In this model, core and peripheral values (i.e. values and practices) are considered as critical components in the definition of culture, integrated with the perspective of various cultural levels, including supranational, national, professional, organizational, and group. Core values are defined as enduring beliefs on preference for a certain mode of conduct; and peripheral values are acquired through social learning at the workplace which is built upon consistent core values [9]. In the IT field, the studies of culture focus on the non-technical side of IT interactions and transfers, embracing a series of individuals' workplace behaviour. According to Karahanna et. al [9], such behaviour is a function of simultaneous cultural impact from different levels. And the nature of behaviour would represent core and/or peripheral values to different extents depending on the influential level of culture (see Fig. 1.). Thus, the author believes that the adaptation of the value-based approach would be beneficial in explaining workplace behaviours relating to the cultural interactions in the context of IT offshoring.

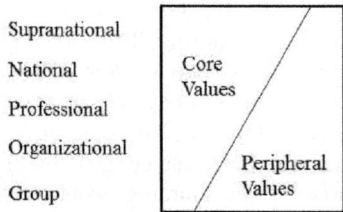

Supranational

National

Professional

Organizational

Group

Core Values

Peripheral Values

Fig. 1. Core and peripheral values [9]

In the IT-culture research field, national culture [10] [11] and organizational culture [12] are still two major streams in the cultural research [5]. For a more concise analysis of literature, this study simplifies the above-mentioned model of cultural values on these two focused levels of national and organizational. In addition, the levels of cultural investigation are introduced as another analytical categorization, including individual, project (group), firm (organizational), and professional. This categorization will be explained in the section of data analysis.

3   Research Methodology

Literature review is adopted as the research methodology in this study to identify emerging culture presence in IT offshoring. In practice, the author followed a similar approach carried out by Leidner and Kayworth [5] in their IT-culture research.

3.1   Literature Search Strategy

The objective of this study is to identify studies in which both IT offshoring and culture are significant themes. In particular, this research aims to investigate culture in IT offshoring, so the subject of the target articles is limited to IT offshoring. In some studies, multiple themes within the IT offshore subject are investigated, with culture as one of the various aspects. These articles are recorded for future usage, but excluded in the analysis scope within this study. Hence, this paper reports only those articles on IT offshoring with a primary focus on the aspect of culture.

As pertinent journal databases would accelerate the identification of relevant articles [13] in the leading journals, the author first conducted a search with such keywords as "IT offshore" and "culture" in several databases with the reputation for quality. Namely, these databases include ABI/INFORM global (ProQuest), EBSCO host, The ACM Digital Library, IEEE Xplore, and The AIS Electronic Library, in which the last two were mainly examined for relevant conference proceedings. The next step is to deploy similar approaches in some specific journals, such as MIS Quarterly, Communication of the ACM, Information Systems Research, Information Systems Journal, Journal of Information Technology, Decision Sciences, and Information Systems Management. The whole search process didn't limit the time span of target articles to be objective on the history of offshoring research.

3.2   Research Sample

After the search process, a total of 83 articles were identified with culture as one of the various aspects in IT offshoring, in which 24 articles were selected with a primary focus on the aspect of culture. Table 1 shows the articles analysed in this study in chronological order, as well as the abbreviation of each article to be referred to in the following sections. A summary on the distribution of the publications across years can be found in Fig. 2.

As shown in Table 1, the selected articles are mainly from academic journals and conference proceedings. Because of the interdisciplinary nature of this topic, some articles from non-IS/IT journals are also included, which focus on the study of people issues.

Table 1. Analysed articles

Year	Authors	Publication outlets
2004	Krishna et al. (Kr) [14]	Communications of the ACM
2005	Wu (Wu) [15]	ACIS 2005 Proceedings
2006	Gorlenko (Go) [16]	Interactions
	Raghuram (Ra) [17]	Human Systems Management
2007	Cohen & El-Sawad (CE) [18]	Human Relations
	Keil et al. (Ke) [19]	Information Systems Journal
	Ramingwong & Sajeev (RS1) [20]	Communications of the ACM
	Wareham et al. (Wa) [21]	IEEE Transactions on Professional Communication
2008	Ang & Inkpen (AI) [22]	Decision Sciences
	Avison & Banks (AB) [23]	Journal of Information Technology
	Beugré & Acar (BA) [24]	Decision Sciences
	Ramingwong & Sajeev (RS2) [25]	2nd IFIP/IEEE International Symposium on TASE
	Winkler et al. (Wi) [26]	Information Systems Frontiers
2009	Gregory et al. (Gr) [27]	Information Technology & People
	Rai et al. (RM) [28]	MIS Quarterly
	Ramingwong et al. (RS3) [29]	22nd Conference on CSEET
2010	Combs et al. (CC) [30]	Human Resource Management
	Coyle (Co) [31]	Antipode
	Hahn & Bunyaratavej (HB) [32]	Journal of Operations Management
	Lowry et al. (Lo) [33]	Information Systems Journal
	Ramingwong & Sajeev (RS5) [34]	2nd IEEE International Conference on ICIME
	Sajeev & Ramingwong (RS4) [35]	The Computer Journal
	Van Marrewijk (VM) [36]	Scandinavian Journal of Management
	Youngdahl et al. (Yo) [37]	International Journal of Operations & Production Management

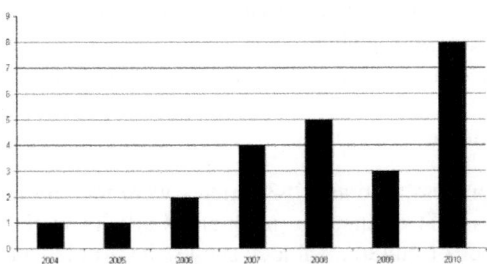

Fig. 2. Distribution of publication years

3.3 Data Analysis

The method for analysis of the selected articles is adapted from a similar study by Leidner and Kayworth [5]. As mentioned before, they have conducted a comprehensive literature review on culture in the context of IS/IT. Thus their method for data analysis should be also valid when narrowing the context to IT offshoring. This method first classified the articles according to their focused level of cultural values, which is organizational and/or national culture. Then, through the detailed review, each article is coded into the following information: methodology, independent, dependent and moderating variables, and relevant findings. This process results in the observation of several culture-related themes studied in the IT offshoring context (Appendix with this information can be requested from the Author). In addition, due to the specific natures of IT offshoring compared to general IS/IT, the author extracted extra information from the articles. This additional information includes model of offshoring, perspective of the articles, and level of cultural investigation. As discussed in the concept of IT offshoring, two models of offshoring are included in this study – offshore outsourcing and captive offshoring. Associated with each model, different perspectives will be adopted in each study. Specifically, in offshore outsourcing, studies will be conducted either from client (usually refers to a company in high-cost countries) or vendor (usually refers to the other company in low-cost countries) perspective; while in captive offshoring, the perspectives can be named as source (headquarter in high-cost countries) and captive (captive centres in low-cost countries). Besides, a neutral perspective is also widely adopted in both models of offshoring. Levels of cultural investigation show the level of studied objects, including individual, project, firm, and professional. This objects' level identification differs from the cultural value focus levels in a way that the studied objects carry the cultural value manifested in their behaviours. For example, the study on an individual employee's behaviour would show the relevant national culture influence; likewise, a project level investigation would possibly observe the organizational culture manifested by the team. These classifications are discussed in the next section of Results.

4 Results

In the sample of 24 articles, 22 observed the cultural values on the national level, one on the organizational level (AI), and another one on both national and organizational levels (RM). Meanwhile, the investigations were made on various levels including professional, firm, project and individual. It is interesting to notice that most of the articles have examined the culture value and carried out the investigation both on a single level. There is only one exception (RM) out of the whole sample, which has carried out a multi-level research investigated at both individual and project levels and on both national and organizational culture.

Six IT offshoring-culture themes were identified, including (1) relationship management, (2) cross-cultural communication, (3) offshoring decisions, (4) individual effectiveness, (5) offshoring evolution, (6) cultural intelligence. Within each of the themes, active interactions occur between culture and offshoring. Table 2-4 provide summaries of this review by mapping the sample into the six themes, across the methodologies, offshoring models, and investigation levels.

Table 2. Sample mapped by cultural themes and methodologies

Theme	Interpretive research	Case study	Conceptual research	Laboratory experiment	Conversation analysis	Field study	Survey	Archival statistics analysis
Relationship management	Kr	Wu, CE, Wi, VM	BA			RM		
Cross-cultural communication		Wa	RS1, RS2	Ke, Lo	AB		RS3, RS4, RS5	
Offshoring decisions	Go	Co						HB
Individual effectiveness	Ra						CC	
Offshoring evolution			Yo					
Cultural intelligence		Gr	AI					

Table 3. Sample mapped by cultural themes and models of offshoring

Theme	Offshore outsourcing			Captive offshoring			Other[1]
	Client	Neutral	Vendor	Source	Neutral	Captive	
Relationship management	Wu, Wi	Kr, BA	RM		CE, VM		
Cross-cultural communication	RS1, RS2	Wa, AB	RS3, RS4, RS5				Ke, Lo
Offshoring decisions	Co			Go, HB			
Individual effectiveness	Ra		CC				
Offshoring evolution						Yo	
Cultural intelligence		Al, Gr					

---

[1] The category "Other" refers to the study on culture in the general context of IT offshoring, which didn't explicitly direct to any models. In this research, both articles using laboratory experiment fall in this category.

Table 4. Sample mapped by cultural themes and level of investigation

Theme	Professional	Firm	Project	Individual
Relationship management	Kr	BA	Wu, Wi, VM RM	CE RM
Cross-cultural communication	RS1, RS2, RS3, RS4, RS5, Lo		Wa, Ke	AB
Offshoring decisions	Go, HB		Co	
Individual effectiveness				Ra, CC
Offshoring evolution	Yo			
Cultural intelligence		AI		Gr

5 Discussion

As the research methodology in this study is simplified from a systematic literature review, the 24 articles selected for this study should be only considered a representative sample rather than exhaustive data. However, the search process has been objective, and without limitations to any specific time period or categories within the IT offshoring context. Therefore, the results presented in the previous section can be considered as valid and effectively representative to manifest the relevant research actuality and trends. Observing through the sample articles, the periodical distribution in Fig. 2 shows a rough but clear trend of increasing research attention on culture in IT offshoring. It also exhibits that this topic is considerably new compare to the general IT/IS research, with all the publications issued after the millennium. The following discussion will be conducted around the six themes identified in the results, and the mapping results across those themes.

5.1 IT Offshoring-Culture Themes

Six IT offshoring-culture themes have been observed in this review. A brief explanation on each of the themes is necessary for the understanding of their relevancy to the topic.

Theme 1: Relationship Management. Relationship management contains a broad spectrum of activities and phenomena in offshoring operations. Two sub-levels were identified, namely inter-organizational relationship (Kr, Wu, Wi, BA, RM, VM) and interpersonal relationship (CE). The relationship quality of both sub-levels is considered as critical success factors of IT offshoring, and it drives the further development of an offshore cooperation. Meanwhile, almost all the articles on this theme identify the significant influence of cultural differences on the relationship quality, or directly on IT offshoring success.

Theme 2: Cross-Cultural Communication. A good communication quality within a cross-cultural background is also considered as an important factor leading to

IT offshoring success. As argued in the relevant articles on this theme, communication quality is directly affected by the difference of cultural values, and it in turn influences the whole offshoring process. Various issues are discussed within this theme, among which the "mum effect" developed mostly by Ramingwong and Sajeev is an emerging and prominent topic (RS1, RS2, RS3, RS4, RS5, Ke).

Theme 3: Offshoring Decisions. Three of the articles discussed under the theme of offshoring decisions, respectively on the question of "offshoring or not" (Go) and offshoring location evaluation (HB, Co). The impact of the culture context is proposed as a decisive consideration in starting an offshore operation.

Theme 4: Individual Effectiveness. This theme seeks to investigate the performance of individual team-members working in an offshoring context. It can be considered together with relationship management as part of offshoring operations. Compared to relationship management, the examination of individual effectiveness is more intrinsic and at a more "micro" level. Individual effectiveness is part of the entire performance of an offshoring operation, and thus is an important aspect of offshoring success. Culture values play a moderating role to determine the influence factor to individual effectiveness, e.g. organizational identification with the client (Ra), or service workers' hope (CC), and further affect the overall success of IT offshoring.

Theme 5: Offshoring Evolution. Youngdahl, Ramaswamy, and Dash (Yo) examined the evolution of offshore operation roles. They argue that the consistent cultural change, together with economic development, will enforce the progression of offshore operation roles to higher levels. Notably, culture is investigated as a variational factor through the evolution of offshoring operations, instead of being fixed and static. This view of culture is also adopted by Van Marrewijk (VM) under theme 1.

Theme 6: Cultural intelligence. Cultural intelligence is a novice theme in the management of offshoring business. It is embedded in the interaction between offshoring activities and their cultural background. Firm level (Al) and Individual level (Gr) cultural intelligence are both studied as a driving force on offshoring success.

5.2   Sample Mapping across the Themes

Various methodologies were adopted in order to examine the relationship of IT offshoring and culture, and there is also no single choice of methodologies in each of the six themes. Explicitly shown in Table 2, case study is the most utilized methodology, which illustrates to some extent that the existent research is still mostly in the quest of theory building. However, the increasing number of conceptual research can be a sign of advancement towards more mature theories in this area. Meanwhile, the less utilized methodologies, such as conversation analysis and laboratory experiments, are representing examples of exploratory attempts for new paths in this area.

Compared to offshore outsourcing, the studies of captive outsourcing are just at the commencement. According to Table 3, captive outsourcing so far has received less research attention. On the other hand, multiple perspectives are introduced in both models. For example, the vendor perspective received almost equal attention as the client perspective in offshore outsourcing, which is on the contrary to the assumed research tendency to the purchase (client) perspective [6]. Moreover, it is worth noticing that most of the case studies observed offshoring vendors/captive centres from India, and clients/captive sources from western countries. Only one article (Wu) studied a case from the perspective of a Chinese client. Meanwhile, several articles investigated the impact of East Asian (i.e. Korean, Thai, and Chinese) culture through laboratory experiments (Ke, Lo) or survey method (RS3, RS4, RS5). This country-biased research situation is consistent with the global market actuality in IT offshoring, in which offshoring usually takes place unidirectional from western countries to India. However, the rise of the other BRIC countries (i.e. Brazil, Russia, and China) and some other regions (e.g. Eastern Europe, East and Southeast Asia) in IT offshore vendor capabilities is bringing more diversity to the IT offshoring business. In the same way, there would be more demands for offshore cooperation in the emerging countries as well, due to their increasing needs for leading-edge technology. This trend certainly brings more lateral complexity as well as new opportunities to the IT offshoring – culture studies.

Table 4 reveals multi-level observations in the field, though the cultural value focus shows an obviously tendency to the national level. This is also consistent with the IT offshoring characteristics, which is usually carried out between geographically distant countries. As a result, the national cultural has more significant impact in offshoring than in the general IT/IS context. The research interest on multiple levels (i.e. professional, firm, project, and individual) is correlated with the longitudinal complexity of IT offshoring operations. However, most of the analysed articles perform a single-level investigation. As the only one exception out of the 24 articles, Rai, Maruping, and Venkatesh (RM) have carried out the investigation at both individual and project levels and on both national and organizational culture values. This can be a good example of multi-level study, which guides the research forward to the future.

6 Limitations

Limitations in this literature review mainly lie in the simplified process of literature search. First of all, due to the search criteria, the results of literature only include articles with themes on both offshoring and culture. This approach is practical to filter irrelevant results to the maximum extent, yet it inevitably overlooks certain relevant results. For example, some relevant articles on outsourcing or global software development are left out because the term "offshore/offshoring" is not used in the text. Hence, a comprehensive search needs to modify the search criteria to a more generate level (e.g. including the search results on "outsource/outsourcing", and "global software development"), and then obtain the final sample by manual selection. Then, the selection of literature outlets still needs deeper consideration. Particularly, the selection of specific journals needs reference to certain authoritative rankings, in order not to overlook any important journals in this field. Moreover, the scan of the major journals is also based on keywords search, which again might result in the problem of over-filtering. Instead, scanning the table of contents in each of the major journals can be an alternative to obtain more comprehensiveness. Webster and

Watson [13] suggested include a final step of backward/forward search in the literature identification, in order to determine prior articles cited in the identified sample, and detect articles citing them. This step would ensure the least omission of critical articles. So the lack of backward/forward search can be considered as another limitation in this study. Finally, it would be beneficial to incorporate a broader range of knowledge, e.g. sociology and psychology, into IT offshoring studies, which is also lacking in this paper. Therefore, further effort is needed to refine the provided framework, through future analysis involving a more comprehensive sample of articles, more detailed examination on each of the identified themes, and effective comparison to other existent and relevant frameworks.

7   Conclusion

This paper conducted a literature review of prior IT offshoring research on the aspect of culture. It provides a summary of cultural impacts on offshoring decision, relationship management, individual effectiveness, and offshoring evolution. Meanwhile, it also identified the studied cultural interactions in the background of IT offshoring activities, such as cross-cultural communication and cultural intelligence.

An illustration on the relationship of the six IT offshoring-culture themes is provided by Fig. 3. The interactions within the cultural background embrace and affect the IT offshoring development, which involve both cross-cultural communication (theme 2) and cultural intelligence (theme 6). The rest four themes constitute the IT offshoring lifecycle, including offshoring decision (theme 3), offshoring operations (theme 1 and theme 4, i.e. relationship management and individual effectiveness), and offshoring evolution (theme 5). They formed a close loop, advancing the development of IT offshoring with positive feedback. This figure reveals that the whole IT offshore lifecycle is immersed in related culture environment, and hence impacted by the interaction of different culture values. This provides a practical framework for future research.

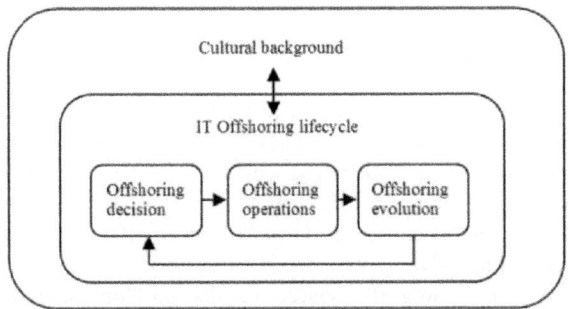

Fig. 3. Summary of IT offshoring-culture research

In addition to this framework, some more conclusions are summarized below:

– In IT offshoring study, culture is mainly studied at the national level. However, the investigation on organizational level is also scarcely identified. More integration of these two levels is desired in the future studies, as multi-perspective and

multi-level analysis would result in a more holistic view on the cultural impact on IT offshoring.
- The most common methodologies in general IT/IS research are also effectively applicable in IT offshoring research. Although the most utilization of case study reveals the novelty of this research field, the increasing usage of conceptual research shows the progress in the quest of theory-building. Some identified new methodologies have broadened the view for future research.
- The existent literature has been largely biased on the investigated countries, which is in consistency with the one-way actuality of IT offshoring from western countries to India. To be in pace with the global economic transformation, more research attention is needed on other emerging countries in IT offshoring business.
- The model of captive outsourcing so far has received less research attention than offshore outsourcing. However, the multiple perspectives within each model are almost equally studied, illustrating the eclectic nature of IT offshoring-culture study.

In conclusion, this literature review provides IT offshoring researchers with a summary of prior research on the aspect of culture, and the results are also valuable for practitioners to examine cultural impact in their own IT offshoring activities. Most importantly, the review encourages more research attention on the relevant topic in the future.

References

1. Carmel, E., Tjia, P.: Offshoring Information Technology. Cambridge University Press, Cambridge (2005)
2. Ravichandran, R., Ahmed, N.U.: Offshore Systems Development. Information & Management 24, 33–40 (1993)
3. Smith, M.A., Mitra, S., Narasimhan, S.: Offshore outsourcing of software development and maintenance: A framework for issues. Information & Management 31, 165–175 (1996)
4. Khan, N., Fitzgerald, G.: Dimensions of offshore outsourcing business models. Journal of Information Technology Cases and Applications 6, 35–50 (2004)
5. Leidner, D.E., Kayworth, T.: Review: A Review of Culture in Information Systems Research: Toward a Theory of Information Technology Culture Conflict. MIS Quarterly 30(2), 357–399 (2006)
6. Jahns, C., Hartmann, E., Bals, L.: Offshoring: Dimensions and Diffusion of a New Business Concept. Journal of Purchasing & Supply Management 12, 218–231 (2006)
7. Youngdahl, W., Ramaswamy, K., Verma, R.: Exploring new research frontiers in offshoring knowledge and service processes. Journal of Operations Management 26(2), 135–140 (2008)
8. Straube, D., Loch, K., Evaristo, R., Karahanna, E., Strite, M.: Toward a Theory-Based Measurement of Culture. Journal of Global Information Management 10(1), 13–23 (2002)
9. Karahanna, E., Evaristo, J.R., Srite, M.: Levels of Culture and Individual Behaviour: An Integrative Perspective. Journal of Global Information Management 13(2), 1–20 (2005)
10. Hofstede, G.: Culture's Consequences: International differences in Work-related Values. Sage Publications, Beverly Hills (1980)

11. Hofstede, G., Bond, M.H.: The Confucius Connection: From Cultural Roots to Economic Growth. Organizational Dynamics 16(4), 4–21 (1988)
12. Hofstede, G., Neuijen, B., Ohayv, D.D., Sanders, G.: Measuring Organizational Cultures: A Qualitative and Quantitative Study across Twenty Cases. Administrative Science Quarterly 35, 286–316 (1990)
13. Webster, J., Watson, R.T.: Analyzing the Past to Prepare for the Future. Writing a Literature Review 26(2), xiii–xxiii (2002)
14. Krishna, S., Sahay, S., Walsham, G.: Managing Cross-Cultural Issues in Global Software Outsourcing. Communications of the ACM 47(4), 62–66 (2004)
15. Wu, W.: Carrying out Contract Successfully Ends Up with an IT Outsourcing Failure: Relationship Management Cases of IT Outsourcing in a Cross-Cultural Context. In: ACIS 2005 Proceedings. Paper 23 (2005)
16. Gorlenko, L.: The Moment of Truth: How Much Does Culture Matter to You? Interactions 13(2), 29–31 (2006)
17. Raghuram, S.: Individual Effectiveness in Outsourcing. Human Systems Management 25, 127–133 (2006)
18. Cohen, L., El-Sawad, A.: Lived Experiences of Offshoring: An Examination of UK and Indian Financial Service Employees' Accounts of Themselves and One Another. Human Relations 60(8), 1235–1261 (2007)
19. Keil, M., Im, G.P., Mähring, M.: Reporting Bad News on Software Projects: The Effects of Culturally Constituted Views of Face-saving. Information Systems Journal 17, 59–87 (2007)
20. Ramingwong, S., Sajeev, A.S.M.: Offshore Outsourcing: The Risk of Keeping Mum. Communications of the ACM 50(8), 101–103 (2007)
21. Wareham, J., Mahnke, V., Peters, S., Bjorn-Andersen, N.: Communication Metaphors-in-Use: Technical Communication and Offshore Systems Development. IEEE Transactions on Professional Communication 50(2), 93–108 (2007)
22. Ang, S., Inkpen, A.C.: Cultural Intelligence and Offshore Outsourcing Success: A Framework of Firm-Level Intercultural Capability. Decision Sciences 39(3), 337–358 (2008)
23. Avison, D., Banks, P.: Cross-Cultural (Mis)communication in IS Offshoring: Understanding through Conversation Analysis. Journal of Information Technology 23, 249–268 (2008)
24. Beugré, C.D., Acar, W.: Offshoring and Cross-Border Interorganizational Relationships: A Justice Model. Decision Sciences 39(3), 445–468 (2008)
25. Ramingwong, S., Sajeev, A.S.M.: A Multidimensional Model for Mum Effect in Offshore Outsourcing. In: 2nd IFIP/IEEE International Symposium on Theoretical Aspects of Software Engineering, pp. 237–240 (2008)
26. Winkler, J.K., Dibbern, J., Heinzl, A.: The Impact of Cultural Differences in Offshore Outsourcing – Case Study Results from German-Indian Application Development Projects. Information Systems Frontiers 10, 243–258 (2008)
27. Gregory, R., Prifling, M., Beck, R.: The Role of Cultural Intelligence for the Emergence of Negotiated Culture in IT Offshore Outsourcing Projects. Information Technology & People 22(3), 223–241 (2009)
28. Rai, A., Maruping, L.M., Venkatesh, V.: Offshore Information Systems Project Success: The Role of Social Embeddedness and Cultural Characteristics. MIS Quarterly 33(3), 617–641 (2009)

29. Ramingwong, S., Sajeev, A.S.M., Inchaiwong, L.: A Study on a Multidimensional Model of Mum Effect among IT Students. In: 22nd Conference on Software Engineering Education and Training, pp. 69–76 (2009)
30. Combs, G.M., Clapp-Smith, R., Nadkarni, S.: Managing BPO Service Workers in India: Examining Hope on Performance Outcomes. Human Resource Management 49(3), 457–476 (2010)
31. Coyle, A.: Are You in This Country? How "Local" Social Relations Can Limit the "Globalisation" of Customer Services Supply Chains. Antipode 42(2), 289–309 (2010)
32. Hahn, E.D., Bunyaratavej, K.: Services Cultural Alignment in Offshoring: The Impact of Cultural Dimensions on Offshoring Location Choices. Journal of Operations Management 28, 186–193 (2010)
33. Lowry, P.B., Zhang, D., Zhou, L., Fu, X.: Effects of Culture, Social Presence, and Group Composition on Trust in Technology-Supported Decision-Making Groups. Information Systems Journal 20, 297–315 (2010)
34. Ramingwong, S., Sajeev, A.S.M.: Influence of Culture on Risks in Offshore Outsourcing of Software Projects: A Quantitative Study on Mum Effect. In: 2nd IEEE International Conference on Information Management and Engineering, pp. 401–404 (2010)
35. Sajeev, A.S.M., Ramingwon, S.: Mum Effect as an Offshore Outsourcing Risk: A Study of Differences in Perceptions. The Computer Journal 53(1), 120–126 (2010)
36. Van Marrewijk, A.: Situational Construction of Dutch–Indian Cultural Differences in Global IT Projects. Scandinavian Journal of Management 26, 368–380 (2010)
37. Youngdahl, W.E., Ramaswamy, K., Dash, K.C.: Service Offshoring: The Evolution of Offshore Operations. International Journal of Operations & Production Management 30(8), 798–820 (2010)

Author Index